MY AUNT LOUISA AND
WOODROW WILSON

MY AUNT LOUISA

AND

WOODROW WILSON

❖

MARGARET AXSON ELLIOTT

❖

CHAPEL HILL

THE UNIVERSITY OF NORTH CAROLINA

PRESS

To E. E.

And to the memory of E. A.

CONTENTS

vii

PART I

❖

My Aunt Louisa

CHAPTER I

SEATED next to me at our hostess' long dinner table
was a distinguished American author who had written
a life of Woodrow Wilson. We spoke of the book.

"Why did you call President Wilson a bad tempered
man?" I asked.

He glanced up surprised. "What should I have said?
Quick tempered?"

"No," I replied. "He wasn't temperish at all. And I
know what I am talking about," I added, seeing the uncon-
vinced look on his face. "I was his wife's little sister. I
grew up in his household, and I never saw him in a temper,
or peevish or irritable. *Angry*, yes!" I began to laugh, remembering an occasion when my beau of the moment had
kept me out on a canoe picnic later than the Princeton of
that era thought seemly. I had managed to slide in the
back door, and so to bed, but Woodrow had his innings
next morning. Oh yes, I had seen Woodrow Wilson angry!

The distinguished author let out a fat chuckle. "Listen!" he said. "All the world has written of Wilson. His wife wrote of him, and his daughter, his secretary, members of his Cabinet, most of his friends, and all of his enemies. Why don't you tackle him from the point of view of the in-laws?"

"And produce another 'Me and Woodrow Wilson' book?" I scoffed. "You all did it," I continued. " '*I* said to the President.' '*I* convinced the President that *I* was right.' Me and Woodrow Wilson!"

I scoffed, but as a matter of fact, it was that "Me and Woodrow" angle that finally made me follow the distinguished author's suggestion. Woodrow Wilson was a many-sided man, and every biographer, of necessity, had portrayed the special facet with which he himself happened to be familiar. And there, all unnoted, were the facets which Woodrow showed chiefly to the "in-laws," the sizeable group that at one time formed so large a part of Woodrow's and Ellen's lives. Certainly some one should "tackle him from the point of view of the in-laws!"

As I think back to the in-laws, it is not surprising that my Aunt Louisa should loom first in my mind. She was the most important figure in the world of the child Margaret, just as later, when the boundaries of that world were broadened, Woodrow himself became the most important figure. Moreover, it was my Aunt Louisa who first spoke to me of my brother-in-law. Not that she ascribed to him any great personal significance! Lacking a divining rod, she saw no vision of a future in which he would stand out pre-eminent. To her he was always "Elly Lou's husband," or, even more often, "Dr. James Woodrow's nephew," and as such she always referred to him.

However, as I realize now, there was another reason for this linking of the two in my mind, and that was the striking similarity between them, a similarity that transcends their equally striking differences. They belonged to different generations, but both generations were of the Civil War period, with the moulding and sharpening of character which that entailed. They were children of Presbyterian ministers, northern ministers, who had moved South and had become more southern than the Southerners. They grew up in small southern towns, in the fierce light that in all such communities beats upon the Manse. They were disciplined by their preacher fathers, and still more by the concepts and prejudices of their fathers' churches. Woodrow's mother, born in Scotland, had been christened Jessie, but the small, strait-laced community in Ohio to which her father brought her felt that the Biblical name "Jesse" was a man's name, and should not be borne by the Minister's *daughter*. So during all her childhood the girl was called "Jennie."

My Aunt Louisa never emerged from the narrow environment in which fate had placed her. Woodrow, of course, did emerge. He became an intellectual of the first rank, a scholar, a wit; a distinguished writer and speaker; the president of a great university; governor of a great commonwealth; President of the United States. On the surface nothing could be more unlike than the lives of these two. But beneath the surface were the two Puritans, the two Calvinists, disciplined and trained by the same rigid faith. Certain habits of thought, even certain words, were woven into the fabric of their characters. Did one of them use the word covenant, for instance, the other knew at once what he meant. Not a bargain, not a contract, not an agreement, but a religious term, the fighting word which had summoned their forebears to battle.

For at bottom they were both Covenanters. They might not enjoy a fight, but when conscience demanded it, they fought grimly. With Woodrow the grimness was overlaid by a certain gaiety of spirit, by his easy, graceful manner, by his scholarship. But to the end of her life, my Aunt Louisa remained the stern, dour Puritan.

If there be those who think of New England as the grim home of the Puritan and vision the whole South as the happy hunting ground of Laughing Cavaliers, I assure them here and now that they never knew the South of my Aunt Louisa, nor the town Illyria,* which was a concentrated essence of that South. In this narrative of the in-laws I have pictured only Illyria, that being the town which I myself knew best, but I might just as easily have chosen any one of the half dozen or so communities in which Woodrow spent his boyhood. They were all more or less of a pattern.

The center of Illyria was a dusty, pock-marked Square,

---

*Don't look for "Illyria" in your postal directory. It is a combination of all the small southern towns I knew so well, in particular of the two towns which are associated in my mind with my Aunt Louisa and the Colonel's wife Meena.

and at the center of the Square stood the old red brick, white-trimmed court house. Sparse grass and a few big maple trees saved the Square from stark bareness, but the one-storey offices and stores that lined its four sides grilled and sizzled in the relentless southern sun.

From the Square, like the spokes of a wheel, radiated five or six unpaved, almost treeless streets, and at the end of one of those long dusty streets, just before it petered out into a country road, stood the rambling white house of my Aunt Louisa, outside the town limits but by no means outside the town. For at this period of her life, my Aunt Louisa might almost be said to have *been* the town.

She was a tall, angular, unbelievably erect woman whose spine had never known the feel of the back of a chair. Her graying brown hair, clamped into an uncompromising bun at the back of her head, was parted in two smooth bands on her forehead and shaded eyes of a clear vivid blue which always surprised one by their look of deceptive mildness. For my Aunt Louisa was not mild! The evil doer, made unwary by those bland blue eyes, was apt to overlook the grim mouth and square chin, and be brought up with a jolt which would have made running one's head into a stone wall seem like the playful pat of a kitten.

She had had need of hardness in her life, had my Aunt Louisa. Her father had been, in the southern phrase, an Eminent Presbyterian Divine, which meant that he was a minister of distinction and learning. But a Presbyterian minister of those days, however distinguished, received only a small salary; and Louisa had been the oldest of the

Minister's six children. How much that had meant of managing and contriving, of helping with the younger children, and "making things do," only Louisa herself could have told and, needless to say, she didn't tell. Added to the rest, Louisa was a plain girl, lacking any touch of the beauty that might have softened her lot. Once a member of the church spoke of her as "homely," and Louisa, poor deluded little mortal, overhearing it, almost burst with pride thinking that the woman meant a girl who loved her home.

After Louisa came four boys, Thomas, William, Henry, and Robert. And then at the end, another girl, Margaret, destined to be the mother of Ellen Louisa, who became Woodrow Wilson's wife. Margaret was much younger than the youngest of the boys, so much so that the church ladies dubbed her an "afterthought." Times were easier then, the Minister's salary a bit larger, and Margaret was born to a softness which Louisa had never known. Moreover, by some trick of fate, the child was endowed with authentic, ravishing beauty. Great lustrous gray eyes, red-brown hair rippling back from a Madonna-like forehead, and a slim body instinct with grace.

Years later when Ellen, a young married woman, revisited her childhood home, her old negro nurse stood, arms akimbo, and looked at her. "Youse a right smart looking gal, Miss Elly Lou," she pronounced at last, "but yo' caint hold a candle to yore Ma. Milk an' roses, she wuz. Yas'm, milk an' roses!"

The four brothers, of course, adored their little sister.

The mother tried her best not to spoil her, but the father, the stern, unbending Minister, didn't even try. He surrendered unconditionally, made the little girl his companion; took her with him on long drives into the country behind the fast horse which was the one luxury he allowed himself. He was a brilliant, irascible man, with a temper which, as Woodrow often described it, was "fixed on a pivot, ready to turn in any direction." But this daughter of his middle years never saw that temper. To her he was all tenderness and love, whereas the other children, if not actually afraid of him, stood in awe of his unrelenting discipline.

The Minister was a famous preacher. When it was known that Dr. Nathan Hoyt was to preach in Synod or Presbytery, the church was sure to be crowded. More than a generation later, an old, old lady spoke to me of those sermons.

"He showed us the fires of Hell," she said, "and then he swept our souls up to the gates of Heaven."

His congregation, accustomed to him in this role, must have been astonished to see him caught and held captive by the charms of a baby! Samson shorn of his locks!

But of all the child's adorers the most passionate, albeit the most silent, was her "homely" sister Louisa. The grim Calvinist religion, compounded of suppressions and repressions, prevented her from giving voice to her adoration, but undoubtedly the love for her little sister developed a love for all children which was to influence Louisa's whole life. For, visiting in a near-by town, she met a young widower with three small sons and, against all her family's objections, married him.

There was no reason for the family to object. The young widower was a man of the highest character, well-to-do, owner of a smallish but prosperous plantation. But—and this was the crux of the whole matter—he was a Baptist, which to that Calvinist-Presbyterian community meant next door to nothing at all. But Louisa closed her mouth and married him, becoming the stepmother of the three small boys and mistress of the plantation with its dozen or so slaves.

Some time later, the lovely Margaret, although much too young to marry, did marry. As might have been expected, her choice met with the full approval of her parents. The young man was the son of another Eminent Divine in the southern part of the state, a family friend of long standing. He himself was all that could have been desired, recently ordained to the ministry and now occupying his first pulpit. A strikingly handsome young man, dark as Margaret was fair, tall, with a certain elegance of movement which fluttered the feminine hearts of his congregation. Fortunate, thrice fortunate, Margaret!

Children were born to the two sisters, and here an interesting fact is noted. Louisa had a husband, a father, and four brothers, but when her son was born she named him, not for one of those, but for her brother-in-law, Edward. Warren, her husband, was a jocund man, red-faced, stockily built, a lover of laughter. Louisa's Puritan soul never quite accepted that free, Baptist laughter. She cared deeply for her husband but every instinct urged her back to the Calvinist fold which she had left and to that noble incarnation of Calvinism, her sister's husband.

Life seemed set fair for the two sisters and their young families; and then after long threats and mutterings, the South seceded from the Union. It was war now, civil war. Louisa's husband, her four brothers and her brother-in-law all joined the Confederate army and she was left alone on the plantation with her children and the slaves.

Her life during the next four years was that of thousands of southern women, and must have made the early days in her father's manse seem like riotous luxury. Children and slaves to be fed and clothed when there was little food and no cloth for garments. Crops to be planted when there was no seed, and the mules and horses had been taken for the army. Sick to be tended, and no medicine. The North had placed an embargo on all drugs, and no quinine could be obtained even when the dreaded chills-and-fever struck viciously. With a couple of wise old slave women, Louisa would go out into the fields and woods, dig roots and pick herbs, and concoct her own remedies. Probably from this period dated her scorn of the medical profession which was so marked in her later years. She too had been a practicing physician and no doubt knew how valueless were their nostrums.

With Lincoln's Emancipation Proclamation Louisa drew a long breath of relief. "I felt that it was I, not the slaves, who had been freed," she remarked.

But unfortunately it didn't turn out that way. A few of

the slaves, it is true, vanished into the wilds of the North, following the will-o'-the-wisp, Freedom. But most of them clung to the plantation. They had been born there; it was home. Why should they bother to leave it? So the heart-breaking struggle to feed and clothe and protect must continue. It was now that Louisa's gaunt grimness assumed permanent form.

Sherman marched to the sea leaving destruction in his wake. The plantation's big house was stripped bare, then burned. Telling of it later Aunt Louisa said that the officers had been courteous, seeming to regret the necessity, but that a soldier had scooped up small Edward's pitiful make-shift toys and smashed them. "It was quite unnecessary," she said with her usual habit of understatement. "The child was doing him no harm." The furniture, of course, burned with the house; but old Dan, the negro houseman, had sneaked out the silver, rowed across the river, and buried it in a mud bank on the opposite shore. Later he retrieved it and brought it to the cabin in the slave quarters where Aunt Louisa and her children were now living.

The war ended at last. General Lee surrendered at Appomattox and the soldiers came trickling home. Not all of them, of course. Warren himself was a prisoner in the North, and his eldest son had been killed. The three small stepsons who had been so potent a reason for Louisa's marriage to their father had enlisted in that incredible army which in the last months of the Confederacy was so largely made up of boys. Now one of them was dead and the second boy, young John, not yet nineteen years old, returned a

man grown. He looked at the desolate plantation and re-
belled. He had known life at high pressure, and couldn't
settle down to grubbing in the ground like a field hand.
Accompanied by his younger brother, the sixteen-year-old
Peter, he departed for the fabulous West, leaving behind
a hastily scrawled note: "Dere Ma. We're off, me and Pete.
This country's no good any more. Ile rite you when we get
settled out West." (Louisa had never been able to teach her
young stepsons to spell!)

Close on their departure came the carpetbaggers, a worse
visitation than the soldiers. One of them looked at Louisa's
ruined plantation and took it. He took the negroes, too,
promising them that unheard-of thing, cash money as
wages. They apparently made no objection. After all, they
would still be on the plantation, wouldn't they? and that
was still home. But three of the house servants refused to
be hired, old Dan, Mammy Vina his wife, and Cindy their
young daughter. The carpetbagger tried to bully them, but
Aunt Louisa faced him down, her blue eyes smouldering
beneath the thick dark brows, her mouth one grim straight
line.

"These three go with me," she said in that deceptively
mild voice which yet managed to repel all opposition.

The carpetbagger took one look at the gaunt, hard face
and beat a retreat. "All right, Ma'am," he said loftily.
"They wouldn't be no good to me, two wore out old niggers
and a bitch of a gal."

Probably Louisa herself would have been glad to do
without them. Three extra mouths to feed, three extra

bodies whose nakedness must be covered. And with what! But they were her people who had chosen to stay with her, and she must help them. Old Dan wrapped the silver in a tow sack, stowed it in a wheelbarrow beneath a roll of blankets, a miscellaneous collection of garments and a hamper of foodstuffs, and they started out on the ten-mile trek to the town.

There were six of them now, Louisa, the three negroes, and the two children, little Edward and the baby Lulie. Louisa and Mammy Vina took turns carrying the baby while small Edward rode on the wheelbarrow except when, feeling that he was now the man of the family, he demanded to be put down. The four grown-ups were used to hard work but not to walking, and with their makeshift shoes, it was a long, hard, dusty tramp, that forlorn Flight from Egypt.

It took them the better part of three days. The first night they spent in a last year's corn field, crouching beneath the yellowing stalks. The second night they came to another plantation where the house had been sacked but not burned, and they found shelter in the ghostly darkness of the big drawing room, not daring to strike a light, even if they had not been conserving their meagre supply of matches. Fearful of wandering bands of marauding soldiers, they took turns standing guard on the front porch, but the night passed without incident, and on the third day, half-starved and with feet raw with blisters, they reached Illyria.

Even then the prospect looked dreary enough. The

little village, poor at its best, had been wrecked by Sherman's soldiers. Everywhere Louisa saw half-burned houses or chimneys marking where houses had once stood. But on the outskirts of the town were the warehouses where Warren and the other planters had formerly stored their cotton, and in the gaunt emptiness of one such storeroom Louisa tucked away her small family. Other families had also sought refuge in the warehouses and among them Louisa found a few acquaintances as well as others whom she would have preferred not to know. But this was no time for squeamishness. The refugees pooled their scant supplies, the elders sacrificing themselves for the children, and somehow, by hook or crook, they managed to keep alive.

Here it was that Warren, Louisa's husband, found them when, having been freed from a Yankee prison, he at last made his way home. Seven of them now, five grown-ups and two children to be fed and clothed, and still the haunting question—with what? I rather fancy that even Uncle Warren found his laughter stilled.

But he was a resourceful man. He had come through the war without wounds and although the northern prison had sapped his strength, it came back in leaps and bounds now that he found himself once again on his native soil. He explored the near-by fields gathering up seedlings that had sprouted from seed dropped after last year's harvest. He spaded up the ground back of the warehouse and planted an embryo garden. It was spring, and the children in their scanty garments were in no danger of freezing. He and Dan tore down an old shed and with part of the lumber divided the warehouse into four rooms—one for himself and Louisa; one for the two children; one for cooking and eating; one at the end for the negroes. With what was left of the lumber he fashioned odds and ends of crude furniture. Later, he reflected, things would be better. It was a bountiful land, and when full summer touched it, there would be wild berries in the hedgerows, and the fruit trees that had escaped the Yankees would give of their fruit.

They were still living in the cotton warehouse when Sally, Louisa's last child, was born, and her father dubbed her the Boll Weevil. But Sally didn't remain a boll weevil, for one day Warren had a brilliant idea.

Standing on the board sidewalk, idly watching the cobbler fashion a pair of shoes from a bit of canvas and wooden soles, Warren remembered a cow which belonged to one of the townsmen and which after a sudden and mysterious sickness had died only this morning. The owner had been lamenting the fact that he dare not eat the flesh of a cow dead of disease, but that wouldn't affect the hide materially. Warren got possession of the beast by promising to bury the carcass. He stripped off the hide, scraped it and pegged it out to dry. And then he engaged the cobbler to make it into shoes. They were crude enough, no doubt, badly fashioned and hideous, but still they were shoes, the thing which Louisa's war economy had found most difficult to contrive.

Ten years later Warren Wade was the leading shoe manufacturer of the state. He had many things in his favor. The near-by, swift-flowing river furnished the power; the poor whites of the region gave him an unlimited source of labor; and as economic conditions improved, he had less and less difficulty with his raw materials. But taken all in all, it was a clear case of pulling himself up by his own boot-straps.

When his shoe business began to show a profit, he bought for a song a half-destroyed house set in several acres of ground just outside the town limits. Not beautiful to begin with, it was even less so when Warren had added rooms here and there to meet the increasing needs of his family. But, though architecturally a hybrid, the house was always comfortable, with its big, high-ceilinged rooms, wide halls, and broad verandas where before many years passed Lulie would be entertaining her beaux. The kitchen was separated from the house by a passage, roofed and open on one side. On the opposite side were the storerooms and pantries which little by little were beginning to be filled. A few hundred yards away were the negro cabins and beyond them what was left of the barns and stables.

Back of the kitchen was the spring house, the pride of the place. Built with two-foot-thick brick walls, set three feet below the ground level, its brick floor was divided in the centre by a small stream trickling down from an icy cold spring. Here, later, pails of butter would be set deep in the water, and on the shelves against the walls great round pans of milk would thicken to cream.

Louisa had always been a good manager, and after a bit her energy brought results. In her garden rows of vegetables lifted their green heads. Half-dead trees were reclaimed and bore their seasonal fruits. After the first hog-killing, home-cured hams and sides of bacon hung from the storeroom rafters, while winter vegetables—potatoes and turnips and carrots—were dumped into the long-empty bins.

It was during this period that Louisa's influence began to be felt in the town, a strange influence when one considers her almost abnormal reserve. She was always a woman of few words and no lover of frivolities. A devoted church member but taking no part in church suppers or mothers' meetings. She hated strong drink as she would have hated poison, but she made no speeches against it nor allied herself with any temperance organization. So far as I ever heard she served on no committees, and it would never have occurred to her to attend a convention. Yet when the town exercised local option and went "dry," not a man in the community but ascribed it to Mis' Louisa.

That was what they all called her—Mis' Louisa or sometimes Mis' Lou. The young minister, beset by congregational troubles, would make his way out to the one woman who never appeared in the church "parlors." "I'll just talk it over with Mis' Louisa," he would say to his harassed young wife. Old farm women from the back country, worried by unruly husbands and sons, would make a bee line for Mis' Lou. "She's a knowin' lady," they said. "She'll tell us what to do."

Even her husband called her Mis' Louisa, and she, after the fashion of her generation, called him Mr. Wade. As long as I can remember I never heard her use his first name.

More than twenty years had passed since the flight from the plantation. Edward, Louisa's son, had won distinction as an attorney, and already was called "Colonel," the South's title of honor for distinguished lawyers. Lulie had married a young business man of the town and now had a baby of her own. Sally, the Boll Weevil, was a pretty young lady, rather flighty and, her mother thought, too much interested in beaux. A nice family on the whole. A very nice family.

Meanwhile the life of Louisa's sister Margaret seemed to flow in like smooth channels. Her oldest child Elly Lou was engaged to a young professor, Thomas Woodrow Wilson, a nephew of the famous Dr. James Woodrow. Of her two sons, Stockton was still at college and the younger Edward a school boy at home. Margaret at more than forty was still beautiful, slender, and young-looking, with her "milk and roses" complexion. When she found that she was to have another baby, no one felt any particular concern. Margaret herself, in the words of her father's congregation, had been "an afterthought." Here was another.

But this time fate decreed tragedy. The baby was born, a lusty, strong-lunged little girl, but the lovely Margaret died, and Edward her husband, after giving her name to the child, turned his face from life and followed her.

There seems to have been no question but that Louisa should take the baby. To the untravelled Southerners of that period, the North, where Elly Lou now lived, was only one degree removed from the icy wilds of Siberia, no fit place for an infant. So the home was broken up. Stockton

returned to his university and nine-year-old Edward went
to live with an uncle in whose town was an excellent school
for boys. And baby Margaret was carried across the state
in the arms of her Aunt Louisa.

These two deaths, the one following so close upon the
other, struck at the very roots of Louisa's life. In her grim
way, she had adored her sister, born with all the grace and
beauty withheld from Louisa herself. Moreover, though it
impinged not at all upon the very real affection which she
felt for Warren, her husband, Louisa never forgot her first
sight of the man who was to marry her sister. They were
both Puritans, reared in the tenets of Calvinism, and in
his grave young masculine beauty, Louisa saw the apo-
theosis of her religion. His beautiful, controlled mouth,
the grace of his movements which Puritanism could not
quite restrain, his dark, brilliant eyes, all spoke to her of the
Warrior-Saints of a still older religion. She was never a
reader of poetry, but in him she pictured St. George and St.
Michael as the poets had sung of them. Edward, too,
throughout the four tragic years of the Confederacy, had
been a soldier. Afterwards, armed with the Word of God
as he saw it, he had continued to fight until death took
him. As Louisa herself would fight.

Journeying across the state with the baby in her arms,
Louisa must have felt that out of tragedy this at least had
been granted her—to rear Edward's child as he himself
would have wished. Fortunately for her peace of mind, no
soothsayer was at hand to warn her that the pendulum had

swung far out of the orbit of Calvinism, to tell her that this daughter of Edward's, last of a long line of Puritans, had been born a Pagan.

Alas, poor Aunt Louisa!

PART II

❖✦○✦❖

Illyria

CHAPTER II

SOUTHERNERS of those days who visited the North always returned raving about the villages of New England. "So white!" they would say. "So clean!"

It isn't to be wondered at if they lived in towns such as Illyria. The pity of it was that these towns had been laid out originally on an attractive plan. The tree-shaded Square with, if the town were a county seat, the court house in the centre. Four rows of one-storey buildings boxing the Square, and the streets radiating out like the spokes of a wheel. But in Illyria, as in scores of other towns, the attempt to beautify had stopped there. Trees died and no new ones were planted. The hot summers made it difficult to grow grass; so the inhabitants of the town stopped trying. They often had masses of flowers in their gardens, but only bedraggled stretches of moss and weeds instead of lawns. Most of the fine old pre-war houses burned by Sherman had been replaced by mid-Victorian atrocities.

25

The negro quarter, known as Black Bottom, was a scandal and a menace. Flooded out once a year by the spring freshets, the darkeys swarmed back as soon as the water receded, packing themselves like sardines into the mouldy hovels. Epidemics of all kinds started there—diphtheria, typhoid, a motley assortment of fevers—and were carried to the white population by their cooks, housemen, and laundresses.

Somewhat better than Black Bottom were the new streets of the millworkers. Row after row of drab cottages, all exactly alike, each with a few feet of front yard; in the rear, clothes lines festooned with constantly washed but always dingy garments; a heterogeneous mass of discarded household articles. And swarming over the whole section, the pallid-faced children of the poor whites, always untiring breeders.

As the South began to recover from the staggering blow of the war, other manufacturers besides Uncle Warren realized the advantages of Illyria's unlimited power and cheap labor. Northern capital erected two cotton mills; a competing shoe factory was built; and a tannery poisoned the air of the whole region. The river, flowing down swift and clear from the hills, when it reached Illyria was foul with the refuse of the mills. Inside the factories, conditions were probably equally bad because of the unhygienic crowding and lack of ventilation. Child labor was taken for granted. How else, as adult wages mounted, could the owners hope to show a profit? Almost a quarter of a century later, Uncle Warren's daughter-in-law, the "Colonel's" wife, was to lead the crusade against the employing and exploiting of children. Thus do the generations move upward to a clearer conception of man's duty toward his neighbor. It is largely a matter of the period, and Meena in her day was no more generous or public spirited than was Uncle Warren in his.

If this picture of Illyria is repellent, don't think that we felt it. It was *our* town; we were proud of it. We herded chance visitors into our buggies and surreys and drove them around to see the sights. The new city hall, the Opera House, the iron deer in the new mayor's yard. Much later, we took them to see the new water works. But that belonged to a later period when built-in plumbing had displaced the round zinc tubs which were filled by relays of negroes bearing cans of hot water. At first we distrusted the innovation. "Is it healthy?" we asked. "Won't we catch all kinds of diseases?"

Through this town of the early nineties moved the child Margaret, who was I. Sally had a horse and buggy of her own and I adored driving with her around the Square, standing on the leather seat with my hand firmly grasping her shoulder. I knew everybody and everybody knew me. When Sally stopped in front of a store, the owner himself would come out to the sidewalk to say howdy to "Mis' Louisa's little girl." "Have you been a good girl, honey?" he would ask. And I, ignoring all evidence to the contrary, would nod my head vigorously. I *hadn't* been good, and he knew it, and I knew it. Years later, visiting the town as a young lady, I found that the older inhabitants still remembered Freddy and me.

Freddy lived in the big place next to Aunt Louisa's. A year older than I, he claimed his age as an advantage which I obstinately refused to grant. Day in and day out we fought an unending battle, until Cindy, who was supposed to look out for me, let out a despairing wail. "Lawd help us, wuz there ever two such devils as these heah chillun!"

But that was only between ourselves. Let a grown-up approach, and Freddy and I presented an unbroken front to the enemy. And that enemy, sad to relate, was usually my Aunt Louisa. There Freddy could put one over on me. His parents were Catholics, with less rigid notions of child rearing. But Aunt Louisa, the Calvinist, knew nothing of compromise. To her right was right, and wrong was wrong, and she refused to believe that I could not be led into the straight and narrow path of right doing.

The trouble was, I didn't want to be led. I hated church (except when I could march down the aisle in a new frock and hat). I hated Sunday school and prayer meetings and the pastoral calls of the Minister when I had to plump down on the floor in front of a chair and be prayed over. Freddy, too, thought that that was just one too many. As the time for the Minister's visit drew near, Freddy took on the duties of a sentry. Climbing to the top of the gate post, he would keep a watchful eye on the road, and when he saw the black-coated figure approaching, he would give the signal. At that I would be off like a shot, and not even Cindy's gimlet eye ever discovered my hiding place.

That evening, of course, Aunt Louisa would hand out punishment. As her peach switch tanned my bare legs, I would yell bloody murder—"fit to lif' de roof offn' de house," Cindy remarked. But I didn't really mind, for once again I had escaped being prayed over.

Or perhaps, instead of the peach switch, I would be sent to bed without supper and with a portion of the Bible or the Shorter Catechism to learn by heart. That didn't bother me either. I was always what is known in theatrical circles as a "quick study," and, the verses soon mastered, I would lie at ease in the lambent twilight waiting for Cindy to sneak up the back stairs with a tray of contraband dainties— much more and much more delectable than I would have had in the dining room.

Or perhaps, in place of Cindy, Uncle Warren would come creeping into the room carrying a plate of fried chicken and hominy grits and a foaming glass of milk. (Uncle Warren, you remember, was a Baptist and didn't think much of Presbyterian ways.) "I don't like this, Baby," he would say, sitting on the edge of the bed. "I hate to have my baby punished. Can't you be good and do what your Aunt Louisa wishes?" He would look at me with troubled blue eyes, and then suddenly a twinkle would replace the look of anxiety, and a second later I would be in his arms, both of us laughing fit to kill, until Aunt Louisa's stern voice at the door put an end to our laughter —"Mr. Wade! The child has done wrong, and must be punished—"

On one occasion, however, my hide-out strategy went

bad. The old Minister had died and a new, young one had been installed in his place. He changed the schedule of his pastoral calls and Freddy and I were caught napping. Cindy seized me before I had time to disappear, washed my face and hands, yanked the tangles out of my hair, and shoved me into the parlor. I stood just inside the door, sullen and rebellious.

Aunt Louisa evidently had been giving the young Minister points on his new congregation. "The child's two brothers are at school," she was saying as I entered, "and her sister, the oldest of the family, is married to Thomas Woodrow Wilson, a nephew of Dr. James Woodrow."

This was old stuff to me. Dr. Woodrow was high-up in the Presbyterian hierarchy, and I had long ago sensed that Elly Lou's marriage to his nephew had added lustre to the family. The alliance was always mentioned with an expression of decently veiled satisfaction. I waited now for the usual reaction from the new Minister.

The reaction came, but it was not what I, nor (I am sure) what Aunt Louisa had expected. The young Minister smiled. "Before very long," he said, "Woodrow Wilson's name will be far better known than his uncle's."

I looked at the man with a softening of my antagonism. This was the first time that my brother-in-law had been presented to me as an entity, as someone of importance. Not just Elly Lou's husband. Not just the nephew of that vaguely exalted uncle in the background. Later I was to marvel at the Minister's almost unbelievable acumen. How had he, pastor of a small poverty-stricken church in the

South, known enough of a young and as yet obscure professor in a northern college, to be able to envision future distinction?

Children like the feeling of importance, and I was warm-
ing up to the new Minister, when by an evil fate he spoiled
it. The time had come for the pastoral prayer. We knelt
on the floor in front of three chairs, Aunt Louisa and the
Minister with piously closed eyes, I keeping a conspiratorial
glance on Cindy kneeling in the hall just beyond the parlor
door. I paid no attention to the prayer (they were always
the same!) until suddenly I heard my name mentioned—
"We beseech Thee, oh Lord, to bless this child Margaret,
the little orphan sheltered beneath this loving roof—"

I was mad as a hornet, fighting mad! I knew about those
orphans. They lived down by the railroad track in an ugly
red house almost as big as Uncle Warren's factory. I had
seen them when I drove past with Sally, standing around in
their dusty yard, or walking along the road, two by two in a
long row, wearing hideous blue gingham dresses, their hair
sticking out like rat-tails from beneath their stiff straw hats.
I got to my feet with a rush that sent my chair crashing.

"I'm not an orphan!" I bellowed.

The prayer broke off abruptly. They were all standing
now. Cindy rushed in from the hall to grab me. Aunt
Louisa, her devotions so rudely interrupted, was speechless.
The Minister looked dismayed. "I am sorry—" he began.

I stuck out a belligerent chin. "Not an orphan!" I reit-
erated and marched from the room.

Uncle Warren, coming in soon after the Minister's departure, understood at once. "She thought he meant one of those poor little wretches in the County Orphanage. No wonder she was annoyed."

Aunt Louisa looked regretful. "It is too bad," she said. "But she must be punished for her rudeness to the Minister." I was punished!

It is strange that I never learned to hate my Aunt Louisa. That I didn't is perhaps due to a child's innate sense of justice. In my heart I knew when I'd been naughty and that my aunt was well within her rights when she punished me. Also I knew that, beneath her mountain of silence, she really adored me. Occasionally she would look at me, a curious expression on her grim face, and not until years later did I realize that she was seeing in me another little girl, the beloved small sister who had tagged after her, back in their father's manse.

Even stranger than my philosophic acceptance of the punishments was the fact that Aunt Louisa never seemed to realize their utter futility. There was nothing of the sadist in her nature. The little peach switch quite obviously "hurt her more than it hurt me." Also she was by no means a stupid woman and she must have seen that if she drove out one devil, seven others came to take its place. Why then did she persist? Probably only a Puritan could explain it. God? Duty? Spare the rod and spoil the child? Or because she couldn't relinquish the hope that some day the miracle would happen and I would emerge "bathed in the blood of the Lamb"? I don't know.

The truth of it was that my Aunt Louisa and I were

foreordained to contest. "Duty," the polar star of her life, was to me anathema—and in that, I wasn't unique in my generation! What she most loved, I hated. What she feared and distrusted, I loved. Laughter, gaiety, a gay, careless tripping through life. The punishments slid off me like water off a duck's back, leaving my spirit undaunted. To be sure, when my Aunt Louisa reached for the peach switch, I would begin to howl and fly into furious tantrums which sheer obstinacy made me hold on to. Elly Lou, down on a visit from the North, told of a Sunday morning battle centering on the question of a whole or a half apple. She said that the family went off to church leaving me flat on my stomach on the floor, yelling—" 'Course, I'll be dood if you'll dive me that other half apple!" Two hours later, when they returned, I was still flat on the floor yelling for the other half apple. Strange, that Puritans made an issue of such unimportant things.

With Uncle Warren, I was quite different. He was a laughing man and I loved laughter. We had our little jokes and secret passwords. When he came home from the factory at night, I pawed him all over, looking for the toy or bit of candy that was hidden in one of his pockets. Occasionally he would be allowed to take me out to the farm which he owned a few miles up the river in the foothills. A wonderful trip! It took us all day, driving in his buggy behind his team of fast trotters. If it were spring, the dogwood and red bud would be in bloom and purple carpets of wild violets. In the autumn, golden rod, and sumac, and purple jimson weed lined the dusty roads with glory. If the weather were warm, he would let me take off my shoes and socks and strip down to my little "pants and body." The sunshine felt grand on my chubby bare arms.

Uncle Warren knew all the plants and trees, the bird calls, and all the little rustling sounds in the forest. "Listen!" he would say. "That's a rabbit trying to get away from a weasel."

We ate our midday dinner in the farmhouse and then while he talked over things with his farmer I would perch on the bank of the river, clear and swift-flowing and clean here so far above the dirty factories. "Don't fall in," Uncle Warren would say casually.

If Aunt Louisa had so ordered, I would probably have waded in out of plain contrariness and have been dragged out a drowned Ophelia. But because it was Uncle Warren's order, I would sit quietly all afternoon, soaking up the sun, watching the sheen of light on the water, hearing the flop of a fish as it leaped for flies, and the low, sweet voice of the river.

At night when he returned home with a sleeping child in his arms, Uncle Warren would look at my aunt pridefully. "She's been a good girl all day, Mis' Louisa," he would announce. "A regular A-1 good girl!"

I can recall only one occasion when Uncle Warren was really annoyed with me—when Freddy and I stole his razor and expensive shaving soap and lathered and shaved the cat. Even then his wrath didn't last long. He burst into a roar of laughter when he learned that, conscience smitten by the cat's forlorn appearance, we had taken it to the spring house and let it lick the cream from Aunt Louisa's big shining pans of milk. At intervals during the rest of the day I heard him chuckling to himself—"Shaved the cat, by George! Shaved the cat."

The rigors of his Calvinist household left him singularly untouched. The town of Illyria under Aunt Louisa's potent influence, had gone dry. But not Uncle Warren. Every night of his life he had a tall glass of "toddy," ice cold in summer, steaming hot in winter. I told about it in Sunday school one day when the superintendent was harping on the ghastly effect of strong drink on the drinkers. "That's not so," a loud, clear voice from the infants' class announced firmly. "My Uncle Warren drinks toddy every night, and he's not a bit like that."

At the end of the back garden was a one-room house known as the office. Uncle Warren had furnished it after his own taste and there he and his cronies could enjoy a quiet game of whist. They could smoke there, too, which Aunt Louisa didn't allow in the house. But on warm summer evenings he and his best friend, Colonel Saunders (a real *Confederate* Colonel, not a lawyer) liked to tilt their split-bottomed chairs against the two gate posts and puff at their pipes in comfortable companionship. I would climb into my uncle's lap and lean back against the shoulder of his seersucker coat. They didn't talk much, maybe a word or two every half hour. It was enough that they were together.

I like to think of them there in the twilight of the day and of their lives. Two old men, comrades in war, friends in peace.

CHAPTER III

FOR SOME time after that first pastoral call of the new Minister, I shrank from all mention of my brother-in-law's name. It was too closely associated with the unfortunate incident of the orphans. Gradually, however, the unpleasant sensation vanished, replaced by the vicarious pride which the Minister had awakened in me. My best friend, Nell Murphy, told me of a bonus that her father had won from the railroad for which he was shipping agent.

"Yah!" I tilted a derisive nose. "But Brother Woodrow is bigger than old Dr. James Woodrow."

My first recorded contact with my sister's husband had occurred when I was too young to realize its significance. I knew of it only by hearsay—but the family saw to it that I heard. It seems that Elly Lou, expecting a baby, had come south to be with Aunt Louisa who, since the older Margaret's death, had mothered her children.

36

I enjoyed the visit. Every morning I climbed into bed with my sister and shared the delicacies from her breakfast tray, and I must have grown annoyingly cocky as a result of this extra petting. But it didn't last long. One evening after supper I was hustled over to Freddy's house and told I could spend the night, an unprecedented treat of which Freddy and I took full advantage. It speaks well for his mother's neighborly co-operation that she was willing to ride herd on the two of us beneath one roof.

Late the next afternoon Cindy appeared. "Yas'm," she replied to Mrs. Moran's question. "Hit's a girl." Then, darting a mischievous glance at me, "And Somebody's nose is plumb out of joint!"

I touched that somewhat amorphous feature. It *felt* all right; so ignoring the threat in Cindy's words, I went skipping across the two yards and up the stairs to the big front room. "The east guest chamber," Aunt Louisa called it. Elly Lou was still in bed, as I had expected, but beside her, in the place that I had come to consider mine, lay something small and red and squawking.

"It's your little niece, Margaret," Sally gushed. "Isn't she lovely?"

Lovely? That thing with the tuft of black hair on top of its almost bald head, squealing like one of Freddy's puppies? I looked at the adoring faces of the family, all turned in the one direction. I looked at the object of that adoration. Then I lunged forward and slapped that baby with all the force of my strong right arm.

Elly Lou burst into tears; Sally gasped; Aunt Louisa

reached out to seize me. But the young father forestalled her. He drew a chair up to the bed and lifted me into his arms.

"You mustn't do that, Margaret," he said quietly. "She's not much bigger than your doll, but she is alive and you hurt her. You mustn't hurt your baby. You understand, don't you? *You* are your sister's baby, and this is *your* baby. You must take good care of your baby."

I listened, interested in spite of myself, as the quiet voice continued. I began to like the notion. Nell Murphy had been bragging because she had a baby brother and I had nobody. Now I, too, had a baby! I leaned down and touched my niece's small face. "All right," I said, and scrambled out of my brother-in-law's arms.

Jealousy is a poisonous weed and its seeds were there in my heart, but Woodrow's prompt action destroyed them. No doubt the amicable relationship which always existed between my nieces and me was due to the insight of their father who sensed a child's bitter hurt and applied a healing poultice.

My actual memories of the Woodrow of those days are necessarily fragmentary. There is no measuring rod extant to show a child which of her relatives is going to be important. Later, she can only catch glimpses here and there. In one such glimpse I see myself standing in bland indifference while my Aunt Louisa told Woodrow that I had won a Bible as a prize for reciting the Shorter Catechism without a single mistake. I was really and truly indifferent. I already owned three Bibles; so the winning of another was no cause for excitement. Moreover, I knew that Catechism so thoroughly that the reciting of it was a mere matter of routine. No human being existed who could have tripped me up on a question. What did vaguely interest me was the fact that Aunt Louisa seemed to be bragging, she who so quickly squelched any symptom of boastfulness on my part. Sally came into the room and I grinned at her companionably.

Woodrow always declared that he was the miracle of his age in that, though the son of a Presbyterian minister, he had never learned the Catechism, the predestined achievement of every Puritan child. If he wished to quote from it he had to turn to the book. He turned to it now and began asking me questions here and there, at random—"What is the chief end of man?"

"Man's chief end is to glorify God and to enjoy him forever," I replied glibly.

"What is justification?" "What is sanctification?" "What is required in the Seventh Commandment?"

"The Seventh Commandment," I answered, "requireth the preservation of our own and our neighbor's chastity in heart, speech and behavior."

Now, I was a tubby little girl at this time, with a mane of dark hair falling below my shoulders and a round, babyish, peculiarly innocent face. Woodrow's lips twitched as I rolled out the sonorous Mosaic injunction. "By the great horn spoon!" he exclaimed. (All his life that was a favorite ejaculation.) As he closed the book and handed it to me, he said something else which made Sally snort and stifle her laughter in her handkerchief. I looked at them, puzzled. Long afterwards Sally remembered the incident and told me what he had said:

> *"And still they gazed, and still the wonder grew,*
> *That one small head could carry all she knew."*

Another glimpse shows me a summer when Woodrow, Elly Lou, and the children came to spend his vacation at Aunt Louisa's. There were three nieces now, two of them with yellow hair and the very small youngest one with brown. They all wore what the cousins called Kate Greenaway dresses, gathered under their arms and hanging down to their ankles, and poke bonnets trimmed with flowers tied under their chins. When they went out they walked three abreast, holding hands, with a nurse hanging onto the littlest one. The cousins all exclaimed at the charming picture, but what Freddy and I thought wouldn't have been allowed in the mail.

We two long since had escaped the realm of nurses. Cindy, it is true, in addition to her house work, still presided over my baths, combed out my hair, and buttoned me up the back. But for the rest of the time I was free, astonishingly so for a child brought up in the Calvinist tradition. Freddy and I knew every inch of the town by heart, even the streets which we were not supposed to enter. We had the run of two big places with their barns and stables, gardens and orchards, their carpenter shops and blacksmith anvils, their horses and cows and pigs and dogs. Back of the two estates was a wood of dark pine trees, threaded by a small stream. Beyond the wood was a deep gully and beyond that the ground swept upward in open meadows.

All this was our playground and we had no notion of sharing it with what Freddy called "those sissy Yankees." Every morning Aunt Louisa would say, "You must play with your nieces today." "Yes'm," I would reply, and as soon as her back was turned I would vanish. The girls couldn't have kept up with Freddy and me had they tried, and we gave them no chance to try. "Think of 'em trying to climb a tree in them clothes!" Freddy sniffed.

Woodrow had set a deal table in the shade of a big oak tree in the back yard and he worked there during those long, hot summer days. Late one afternoon he saw me trudging home after a glorious free day in the open, and he called to me. Freddy and I had been building a dam in the creek and my bare legs were smeared with mud to my knees. My skimpy cotton frock, so different from those Kate Greenaway creations of his daughters, hung in tatters, my hair was tangled with cockleburs and dead leaves. My brother-in-law grinned. "You've had a whale of a good time, haven't you? Couldn't you let your nieces play with you?"

I shook my head regretfully. I liked this man and I wouldn't mind obliging him, but—"They're no good at our kind of play," I declared. "Freddy says they're sissies."

Woodrow chuckled. "Perhaps Freddy is right," he conceded. "But then again, perhaps his experience is somewhat limited. Take them with you some time and find out."

There my memory of the incident fades. Perhaps we did

take them, perhaps not. I don't remember. But I remember distinctly how much I liked his eyes as he laughed down at me.

When Elly Lou became engaged to Dr. James Woodrow's nephew and family friends asked what he was like, she always replied with a quotation from Wordsworth— *a noticeable man, with large grey eyes.* The description was, and remained, apt. Woodrow, with his big, jutting nose and long jaw, and wide, sensitive mouth, was never a handsome man, but he was always noticeable. His small scrap of a sister-in-law thought then (and still thinks) that his eyes were the nicest she had ever seen. Large and beautifully set, in color a deep, clear gray with no tinge of blue. The color of black ink on gray blotting paper, or of storm clouds piling up in the northern sky. When he looked down at me on that long ago afternoon, they glinted with amusement. He struggled to keep his mouth under control, then suddenly he gave up and flung back his head and laughed, that rare, deep-throated laughter which revealed the inner gaiety beneath his iron-bound, Scottish exterior. It might have hurt my feelings, but it didn't. He was so evidently having a good time. I laughed with him.

I have before me a snapshot taken during Woodrow's first inauguration as President of the United States. He and President Taft are standing side by side on the reviewing stand, laughing at something which had caught their attention in the crowd below. The snapshot might be called a study in laughter. Taft's, the habitual easy laughter of a fat man, his fat stomach a-quiver, his broad round face creased into deep folds. Woodrow's, the rare giving over of his lean hard body to a gust of honest merriment. I smile as I look at the photograph. Once again I seem to be standing beside his writing table in the shade of the oak tree, regretful at having to refuse this nice man's request, listening to his shout of laughter. And once again I hear the voice of the young Minister who first told me that this brother-in-law of mine was somebody important—"Before very long, Woodrow Wilson's name will be better known than his uncle's."

CHAPTER IV

I GREW OLDER and little by little the town Illyria and its inhabitants began to take form as something other than mere appendages to my Aunt Louisa and me. I caught glimpses of lives other than those centering in Uncle Warren's big rambling white house.

Down near the railroad station across from the ramshackle hotel lived one of the few foreigners who, by some twist of fortune, had established himself in this strictly Anglo-Saxon (and African!) community. A fat old German lived there and in his front room maintained a little shop of cheap stationery and cheaper sweets. Once he said something to his wife that I did not understand, this being the first time I had ever heard the sound of a foreign language. "What did you say to her?" I asked.

He looked round at me, amused. "I told her the peppermints are almost gone. She must order more at once."

"Then why didn't you say so?" I demanded. I popped

one of the fat round peppermints into my mouth and turned away puzzled.

"Ho, ho!" he laughed. "The little one thinks all the world should talk English!"

He never forgot the incident. Whenever I appeared he would greet me with a chuckle. "Ha, das kleine englische Mädchen! Come, Mütterchen, now we must talk English!" Once when I was recovering from a childish ailment, he stopped Sally on the street to ask about me and sent me a package of my favorite fat peppermints labelled "For die kleine Engländerin."

How had he come into this small, remote town in the South? I don't know. Perhaps, washed out of Germany during the revolutions of '48, he had drifted here and there until he landed in this safe backwater.

He had prospered in a small way, but the few Irish among us really made good. Freddy's father, Rafe Moran, was one of them. He was a contractor and had built two out of three of the factories which, following Uncle Warren's lead, were now lining the banks of our river. He built, too, most of the shoddy houses for the workers in those factories, whole streets of them, all just alike, looking as though a puff of wind would blow them away. As a matter of fact, when, many years later, a cyclone hit Illyria, those houses vanished in the air like so many bubbles.

Perhaps it wasn't Mr. Moran's fault that those houses were so worthless. He was a good craftsman and would have liked to build honestly. But the wages of the factory hands and the rent they could afford to pay were small, and the owners of the property must needs have their profit. Anyway, Rafe prospered. Long before Freddy and I appeared on the scene he had been able to buy what once had been a fine old place next to Uncle Warren's. He tore down the remnants of the old house—that it had been destroyed by Sherman goes without saying!—and erected in its place a shanty Irishman's notion of what a gentleman's house should be. It was a wonder! Turrets, and pinnacles, and little balconies sprouting all over the structure like shoots from an old potato. And jig-saw lacework wherever he could find anchorage. But Freddy and I had no architectural standards. We thought it was grand! So did all the other neighborhood children when we played hide and seek in the turrets, and climbed from balcony to balcony by means of the lacework.

Another Irishman who had prospered was my friend Nell Murphy's father. He had been a brakeman on the railroad, then conductor, and now was station and shipping agent. Everyone envied the Murphy family because they could go anywhere they liked on "free passes." Mrs. Murphy availed herself of the privilege very often. To our amazement she would ride up to the Capital City just to listen to a concert and come back on the midnight train which was seldom more than an hour or so late. Such a lot of trouble, Illyria thought, just to listen to a concert! Also, and this the town spoke of with bated breath, it was said that Mrs. Murphy read French novels "in the original."

In her pursuit of culture, Mrs. Murphy had a companion in the young wife of the old General. Illyria wondered why so brainy a woman had chosen to link her life with the General's. He had been a great figure in the first years of the Confederacy, General Lee's trusted aide, one of the props to which the South was clinging. A sister of Uncle Warren's named her newborn son for the hero.

Then came the change. A great battle was lost because the General, as the South believed, had failed to bring up the reserves when General Lee ordered. Moreover, during the hideous period of reconstruction, he accepted and held office under the Yankees. That finished him with the South.

"My dears," warned Uncle Warren's sister, "name your children for the illustrious *dead*, for the living may turn into villains!"

I often met the General walking down the street, sometimes with his young wife beside him. A tall, lean old man, with long sideburns, a fringed gray shawl draped across his thin shoulders. When men saw him coming, they turned into the nearest doorway to avoid bowing, or became busily occupied with their horses tied to the hitching rail in front of their stores. Aunt Louisa, seeing this ostracism, looked after the lean old figure with pitying eyes. "Poor old man!" she murmured.

But I felt no pity for the "Traitor," as men called him. I had been told that he was a cousin of my grandmother, my father's mother, and I felt a vicarious shame in his shame. I wanted heroes, not traitors, in my family. "He's a bad man, Aunt Louisa," I protested, parroting what I had heard men say. "He didn't do what General Lee told him."

She looked down at me with a faint smile. "Judge not that ye be not judged," she quoted. "Who can read the secrets of a man's heart?" Strange Aunt Louisa! So rigidly intolerant in small things; so unbelievably magnanimous in big.

There were other tragedies in the town. The son of Aunt Louisa's best friend killed his sweetheart and a man whom he caught making love to her, and was sentenced to life imprisonment. I remember one autumn afternoon when I came upon Aunt Louisa and his mother sitting in Aunt Louisa's parlor. The weather had turned cold suddenly and a raw wind was whistling down from the hills. The old lady looked out at the bleak garden and shivered. "I must get out John's winter flannels tonight and mail them to the prison," she remarked.

She was a beautiful old lady with eyes like brown velvet and a little lace cap pinned to her snow white hair. She and Aunt Louisa looked at each other for a long moment, soft brown eyes clinging to clear, steadfast blue. They said nothing and I was too small to realize the tragic understanding revealed in that look, but I, too, suddenly shivered.

Another tragic figure that came very close to farce was the son of the man who, in the good old days before the war, had owned the place bought by Freddy's father. The son, Ridge Tyler belonged to that truly Lost Generation, the after-the-war Southerners. It was as though the impetus toward life had gone out of them. In feckless apathy they stood aside from important things and watched newcomers, such as Rafe Moran, make fortunes doing work that they themselves might have done. They took small jobs here and there, living from hand to mouth, bitter over their lost glories.

Woodrow spoke of it more than once years afterward. "At first it was commendable in them," he said, "to be willing to turn their hands to anything that offered. But to be willing to continue doing so after more than a generation had passed showed a lack of proper ambition." Then he quoted the Latin motto engraved on an old signet ring, *Honestae studiosus famae*—zealous of honest fame.

Ridge Tyler drove the team of temperamental mules hitched to our one street-car that shuttled back and forth between the Square and the railroad station, which we called the deepot. Sometimes the mules balked and stood like iron statues on either side of the track, while Ridge and his passengers shoved and pulled, or tried to coax them with sugar. Once the brakes failed to work on a hill, the street-car plunged downwards, and the mules ended the ride sitting on the front platform. As an accompaniment to this almost daily circus was Ridge's ceaseless tirade against Rafe Moran who, he declared, had robbed him. It reached the point when no one bothered to listen. The passengers inside would chat unconcernedly with each other while the querulous voice went on and on, vowing vengeance against the damn Yankee interloper—Rafe, who had been born in a cabin in County Clare!

I was only a little girl and I sensed little of these tragedies, large and small. I didn't see the squalor of the

negro section, Black Bottom, nor the teetering on the edge
of poverty of the mill district, nor the complete lack of
civic responsibility of the town. I knew that when Uncle
Warren's factory hands were sick, he sent them doctors and
supplies of food, and that Aunt Louisa's cohorts of pen-
sioners never went away empty-handed. I knew all about
giving to the poor. Aunt Louisa was a firm believer in the
Biblical tithe (though her own personal contributions must
have far exceeded it), and every week she put one cent
from my allowance of ten cents into a box for the poor,
handing over to me the remaining nine pennies.

"The Lord loveth a cheerful giver," she would remark,
with a glance at my sullen face.

I didn't know that all this private charity, which was
not confined to my relatives, was only a stop-gap, that the
town itself should have been responsible for its poor. Boys
and girls went to the bad because of lack of direction. My
older brother told lurid tales of the after careers of his
boyhood associates. One became a famous gambler, to be
shot finally in a gambling brawl. One was an internationally
known con man. One was hanged for murder. One girl,
whose school books he had carried when they were children,
became the Madame of a house in New Orleans.

No one told me anything of the history of Illyria, except,
of course, that Sherman had burned it, until one day Woodrow, out for a constitutional, chanced to overtake me stroll-
ing along a side street, and invited me to go with him.
At about this time he must have been busy with his *Division
and Reunion*, and no doubt his mind was filled with the

story and difficulties of the South. Anyway, almost as though thinking aloud, he began to talk to me about the town in which I lived. I remember very little, naturally, only that he spoke of Indians and their trails through the forests; of early settlers on the banks of the river, floating their goods down stream on rafts; of how a town sprang up and grew and grew until it became Illyria. Then he showed me how Sherman's soldiers had come down from the north, circled the town and burned it.

There at last I was on familiar ground. I had been "raised" on Sherman, so to speak. I told him of Aunt Louisa's plantation and of the mean Yankee soldier who had smashed all the Colonel's playthings. My voice grew shrill with indignation as I thought of my own few but precious toys. Woodrow understood.

"That was war, little Margaret," he said. "A terrible thing!"

I remembered those words when on April 2, 1917, I heard him ask the Congress of the United States for authority to declare war against Germany—"It is a fearful thing to lead this great peaceful people into war."

CHAPTER V

AUNT LOUISA'S lovely old mahogany had burned with the plantation house, and by the time she could afford to buy new furniture, mahogany was out and black walnut was in. Genuine, over-carved, marble-topped black walnut. We all thought it beautiful. A score of years later, it would have seemed atrocious. Now, with the Victorian craze rampant, it would again be much valued.

In spite of the sombre furniture, it was a pleasant house. Aunt Louisa was a good manager and the big rooms were cool and fresh. Every two years she had the outside re-painted shining white with green shutters, and the walls of the rooms "washed" in pale colors. The garden was also attractive. Not for her the slovenly makeshifts which most of the town called lawns. She divided her front yard into beds of various shapes, bordered with low box hedges, and kept the beds filled with flowers. I have since wondered if her Puritan repression did not find outlet in that riot of color. She could make anything grow. "Mis' Lou's sho' got green fingers," Mammy Vina remarked.

I, too, had green fingers and a passion for gardening. When I demanded a bit of ground of my own, it was characteristic of Aunt Louisa that, instead of shoving me off into the back region, she gave me a bed just below the front porch. I was pleased with the location. In addition to its other advantages, it gave me an excellent listening post. Above me on the porch as I unobtrusively dug and weeded, I could hear Aunt Louisa's visitors discussing church affairs, or Lulie's reports on her babies, or Sally quarreling with her beaux. And there one day I heard the seamstress telling Cindy of the revival in the Methodist church. A seemingly unimportant incident, but it led to my "getting religion"— unfortunately not Aunt Louisa's brand.

I badgered the seamstress until she agreed to take me the next evening when all the family was out. It was the third evening of the revival and the visiting evangelist had worked his audience into a fine state of frenzy. When he began calling them to the "mourners' bench," they streamed down the aisle singing, *"There were ninety and nine that safely lay in the shelter of the fold—,"* and shouting, "Lord, I'm a sinner!"

It was a clear case of mob psychology. My muscles began to twitch and my hackles to rise. I stood it as long as I could, then I too joined the rush down the aisle. "Lord, I'm a sinner!" I shouted.

My arrival at the mourners' bench was sensational. At least half of the mourners were Uncle Warren's factory hands. Most of them knew me well and none of them had much use for those snooty Presbyterians. "A ewe lamb snatched from the burning!" one of them cried. The evangelist leaned down and lifted me onto the platform beside him. "A little child!" he sang out. "A little child shall lead them!"

My big straw hat was hanging to my neck by its ribbon; my hair was blowing every which way. I stood there smirking, accepting the adulation, until suddenly a hand grabbed me off that platform and rushed me back up the aisle. "Lord help me! Mis' Louisa—" the seamstress groaned.

Her fears were well founded. Aunt Louisa was home before us, and when she heard what had happened her blue eyes looked at us coldly. She too was religious but not in *that* way. She didn't punish me for the adventure, fearing, perhaps, that punishment would put me off religion altogether. But the seamstress found her services dispensed with.

In her place came Miss Willy, and with Miss Willy came her small daughter Bessie. The pair fascinated me. Miss Willy had jet black hair, what I called a "tight" face, and long, fine, needle-pricked fingers. Bessie was an ash-blonde beauty, and I, worshipper of beauty that I was, haunted the sewing room. When Miss Willy was tired, Bessie and I took turns pedalling the sewing machine. As a reward, she told us of the parties she had gone to as a girl and of the gold ornaments she had worn to the Governor's Ball.

"*Real* gold, Mommie?" Bessie would ask, awe-stricken.

"Of *course*," Miss Willy would reply loftily. "I would-n't have worn anything but real gold." Evidently Miss Willy was born before the day of costume jewelry.

Bessie, a year younger than I, followed me around with gratifying devotion. But I soon began to notice a strange thing. I could play with her as much as I liked on the place, but I wasn't allowed to take her to a friend's house or up to the Square. Once when I was being sent on an errand to the Minister's, I asked if Bessie couldn't go with me. At that Sally, who happened to be in the room, stifled a hoot of laughter, and Aunt Louisa shook her head gravely. "Better not," she said. "The Minister might not like it."

I noticed, too, that although Miss Willy sewed for several of Aunt Louisa's acquaintances, she never worked in their houses as she did with us. Either colored house boys carried the stuff to and fro or else Miss Willy went to her customers for the fittings, and then finished the work in her own home. On such occasions she always locked Bessie in one of the rooms and took the key with her. I felt terribly sorry for Bessie, locked up there by herself; so one after-noon, knowing that this was one of Miss Willy's going-off days, I went down to visit her.

They lived in a three-room house, little better than a shanty, down on the edge of Black Bottom. I had been there before, driving down with Sally with a message from Aunt Louisa, and so I had no difficulty in finding the place. I strolled through Black Bottom, calling greetings to this and that colored woman whom I happened to know. One of them, old fat Maria, who sometimes under-studied our laundress Jinny, eyed me doubtfully. "Looka here, honey," she said, "does Mis' Lou know as how yo's down here by yo'sef?"

"No," I replied. "But she won't mind. She lets me go anywhere I want to."

Maria shook her grizzled head. "Well'm, hit jest ain't fitten. Pears lak that no-count Cindy had oughter look out for yo' better." I grinned. I had chosen a moment when Cindy was busy in the spring house, and I knew I would hear from her later.

Miss Willy's house looked particularly dreary in the blistering afternoon sun. The paint was peeling from the clapboards, and the plants in her attempt at a garden were dying for lack of water. I yoo-hooed for Bessie and when she didn't appear, I circled into the back yard. Then I found her, her small face pressed against a window pane. She was crying and her cheeks were streaked with dirt. "A big colored man wanted to come in," she sobbed. "He said if I didn't open the door he'd break it down. I think maybe he's gone for a hatchet." Her voice reached me distinctly through the ramshackle window.

I looked around. The yard was empty, but standing with one leg lifted, just ready to climb over the back fence, was the biggest, blackest negro I had ever seen. I had never known fear of a negro. Cindy had brought me up. The two house servants, and old Dan and Mammy Vina, living in pensioned ease in their cabin beyond the barn, were my intimate friends. But something told me that this man was no friend. I backed up against the wall alongside Bessie's window and began to yell.

Freddy and I were the champeen yellers of Illyria. When I returned to the town as a young lady, the old inhabitants still spoke feelingly of the strength of our lungs. Now I gave that strength full play. The sound burst out like a factory whistle, reverberated against the house and went ululating across the back yards and through the alleys of Black Bottom. The big negro, startled, lost his balance and fell off the fence, unfortunately for him on Miss Willy's side. For before he could get to his feet and make his escape, old Maria was on him.

It seems that she had followed me at a distance just to keep an eye on Mis' Lou's little gal. At the first piercing note of my yell, she grabbed up a chunk of wood and came running. It took three men to drag the big negro back to his cabin when she was done with him.

Never had I seen Aunt Louisa so upset as when Maria, still holding me by the hand, appeared before her. "Child, child!" she kept saying, and at one moment I thought she was going to burst into tears. That frightened me more than the big negro. I must have done something awful, if it made Aunt Louisa cry.

That night Uncle Warren took me up on his knee and told me that I must never, never again go alone to Black Bottom, and that I must always be in the house before dusk. Awed, I looked up at his kind face, so unwontedly grave, and promised. He told me, too, that after this, when Miss Willy went off on errands, Bessie was to be left at our house.

Children often have a surprising depth of reserve. I had sensed long ago that there was something strange about Miss Willy and Bessie, and now I carefully refrained from asking why Bessie couldn't go with her mother to the other ladies' houses. But years later when I was back on a visit from the North, something reminded me of Bessie and I asked my Aunt Louisa about the mystery. It was just what my adult years had led me to expect. Miss Willy, a girl of good family, had been, in the current phrase, "unfortunate." Her father and mother were dead, and when her brother realized that she was with child, he was done with her. So Miss Willy had her baby and then was left to support it and herself. Her parents had been Presbyterians and Aunt Louisa had insisted that the church members must keep her supplied with work.

"Because of you," Aunt Louisa said, "several of the women blamed me for letting the child Bessie come to the house. But I told them that you were two little girls playing together in all innocence, and that she would hurt you as little as you would hurt her."

I should have known my aunt by then, but I confess that I stared at her in amazement. *Aunt Louisa*, the Puritan, the Calvinist, to have gone so far ahead of her generation! Then, of a sudden, all the Bible verses which she had made me learn came to my aid, and I realized that Aunt Louisa hadn't gone ahead, but back. Back to the Founder of her religion—*And Jesus lifted himself up and said unto the Pharisees: He that is without sin among you, let him first cast a stone at this woman.*

The climax of Bessie's history might have been written by the most romantic of Victorian novelists.

Miss Willy in due course left Illyria to take a position in the linen room of the Capital City's leading hotel, and Bessie in her after-school hours helped her mother with the mending.

One afternoon a young man happened to meet her in an upstairs corridor, carrying a pile of linen. The girl was then about seventeen and a beauty. Her lovely little ash-blonde head above the snowy linen, must have looked like one of Raphael's cherubs floating on clouds. The young man catapulted into love.

He was the son and only child of a big rice planter in Mississippi at a time when rice planters were the aristocrats of the South. His parents learned of Bessie's unfortunate background, but, wise in their generation, they raised no objection. They had always wanted a daughter, they said, and Bessie filled the bill. She was young; she was beautiful; she had the disposition of an angel and could be molded to their desires. She became the petted darling of the plantation.

Later, I was told, she came back to Illyria with her husband and two handsome children. They took the best rooms in the hotel (nothing to boast of, but still the best), hired a carriage and pair from the livery stable, and drove all over the town. The turnout was seen to pause briefly outside the houses to which Bessie as a child was denied entrance. They even, Aunt Louisa said, drove to Black Bottom, and Bessie showed her husband the ramshackle

house where she had lived, and introduced him to old
Maria who on that long ago day had saved us from the
big black man.

Then at the end of the day she presented her family
to Aunt Louisa, and stood, an enchanting, smartly dressed
figure, before the woman who had befriended her.

Aunt Louisa was an old woman then, but still strong and
vigorous. She eyed the little group benignly. "You were a
good child, Bessie," she said. "I hope you are being a good
mother."

CHAPTER VI

IT WAS several weeks after the Methodist revival when I got religion that my Aunt Louisa decided to start me in church work. *Her* church! Of course the church had always been with me, uncomfortably so. I went to at least three services on Sunday and to midweek prayer meeting. I had learned whole chapters of the Bible by heart, and could recite the Shorter Catechism backward or forward or standing on my head. I had won a prize of a Bible for reciting it.

The Sabbath, as Aunt Louisa called it, had become for me a day to be dreaded. In our household no cooking was permitted, and the servants worked most of Saturday preparing the food that would be served cold the next day. All my regular play and diversions were taboo. Only, in the late afternoon, I might go for a sedate stroll in the garden.

But the thing that bored me beyond endurance was the restricting of my reading. I was a precocious reader for my age, and to have *David Copperfield* confiscated and a namby-pamby "Sunday school book" given me in its stead, flung me into a screaming fury that shattered the Sabbath peace. Of course there was always Borrow's *The Bible in Spain*. Aunt Louisa had never read it and labored under the delusion that it told of a proselyting mission to the Spanish heathen. I didn't undeceive her.

But all my religious discipline to date was, in Aunt Louisa's opinion, merely the froth on the sillabub. Now the time had come for me to labor in the vineyard of the Lord, and the task first assigned me was the collecting of the Minister's salary. The same Minister who had so tactlessly referred to me as an orphan. I had borne him a grudge ever since and held aloof from his spiritual ministrations, but now that I was to assume the role of his benefactress, I unbent to him.

Times were still hard in a South not yet recovered from the Great Panic, and church members who had pledged so much a week for the support of the church took to staying away from the services altogether, or omitted to drop their filled envelopes into the collection plate. The harassed Minister, as he usually did in emergencies, went down the road to consult with Mis' Louisa. As a result, a corps of small girls was assembled whose duty it was to round up the defaulters. Aunt Louisa was supposed to lack a sense of humor, but I suspect that she found a grim pleasure in the thought of those weekly encounters between the little girls and the recalcitrant church members.

We all started out briskly enough, but one by one the

others began to drop out, either because the children themselves found other diversions or because their parents grew tired of the black looks from their neighbors. But Aunt Louisa and I were made of sterner stuff. If I had wanted to quit she wouldn't have let me, but I didn't want to. I thought it was fun. Bright and early every Monday morning I appeared at the Minister's dressed in my ruffled linen pinafore and shady straw hat, and was given a list of the collections I must make during that week. Often the defaulting member would be "out" when I first called, but that did him little good. Relentless as the hound of the Baskervilles, I hunted him down until the money he owed was safe in the schoolbag slung across my shoulders.

Once a loutish youth of the town, knowing of my labors (as who didn't!) seized my bag and tried to make off with it. But I, feeling it slipping, grabbed hold of the leather strap and resorted to my usual defense tactics. I began to yell. Lord, how I yelled! A steam calliope would have sounded like a mourning dove in comparison. A crowd gathered instantly and the bag-snatcher, scared half out of his wits, made off down an alley, leaving me, as I liked to be left, the heroine of the occasion. It was lucky for the boy that he wasn't a negro, for in that case he might easily have been lynched.

One Monday morning the name of one of Sally's beaux appeared at the head of my list, a young lawyer of the town, known even in that thrifty community as a tightwad. One of the other children had had him on her list and had visited him week after week fruitlessly, so that when he was handed over to me, he owed a considerable sum. I found him in his law office, one of the one-storey buildings on the south side of the Square, a lanky, lantern-jawed young man with reddish sideburns, sprawled back in his revolving desk chair. He scowled when I bobbed up suddenly beside him. "Well, what do *you* want?"

"Good morning, Sir," I said politely. "I've come for the Minister's salary."

He was about to refuse in no uncertain terms, when all at once something clicked in his brain. "Haven't I seen you before?" he demanded.

"Oh yes, Sir. I'm Aunt Louisa's little girl and Cindy says you're Sally's beau."

Butter wouldn't have melted in my mouth as I, without knowing it, levied this blackmail. For the young lawyer really meant business with Sally and confronted by her small cousin, he dared not refuse to pay up. He eyed me for a long moment in black silence; then he dragged a shabby wallet from his hip pocket (his acquaintances declared he was too stingy to buy a new one) and slowly, reluctantly, as though each bill were a drop of blood squeezed from his heart, he counted out the money he owed.

I counted it, too (I could do that much arithmetic without trouble), and when the full sum was in my hands I popped it into my bag and turned away. But at the door I suddenly remembered the manners in which the Minister's wife had drilled me. I turned back and curtseyed until my hair swung out like a banner.

"Thank you, sir," I said unctuously. "The Lord will reward you."

"Good God!" said the young lawyer.

Elly Lou and her family had been visiting in Savannah and on their way home stopped off for a few days with Aunt Louisa. When Woodrow heard of my summer occupation, he looked from Aunt Louisa to me, the financial support of the church. "A stroke of genius, my dear Aunt!" he observed.

She allowed herself a wintry smile. "The child is only doing her duty," she remarked.

When she had left the room, Sally, with outbreaks of giggles, told him of my blackmailing of her beau. Then, still giggling, she related how I had got religion at the Methodist revival.

Woodrow laughed harder than I had ever heard him. Then he looked at me intently. "Why did you do it?" he asked.

I grinned. Aunt Louisa had taken the affair so seriously that I hadn't seen its funny side before, but now it suddenly struck me as terribly amusing. "I don't know," I chuckled. "I guess it was sort of fun."

Woodrow nodded, a gleam of sympathy in his eyes. He was already a magnificent public speaker, and all such must be endowed with a touch of the histrionic. No doubt he understood, as none of the others, how the crude drama of that revival must have excited me.

It was Woodrow, by the way, who was the cause of my

first seeing a joke, a real joke. I don't remember whether it was during this visit or a later, that he chanced to quote the old definition of a bore—"someone who insists upon talking about himself when you want to talk about yourself." Somehow, I can't imagine why, that doubled me up. I went off into whoops and gales of laughter while the assembled family stared in amazement, and Woodrow observed that his wit had seldom met such an enthusiastic reception.

Before this summer ended, it became evident that my adventure in blackmail had brought a wholly unforeseen result. Because of it, the young lawyer lost Sally, and Sally lost a beau whom she might have hammered into a fairly satisfactory husband. For in his anguish over that shelling out of good money, the young lawyer resorted to the strictest economy, and began, unfortunately, with his weekly box of candy to Sally. Now my cousin was never one to put up with nonsense and by the time her suitor realized that he was playing a mug's game, the second entry had edged into the inside track, and he was out of the race forever.

Sally was never a beauty but she was always pretty. Pretty hair which she put up in curlers every night; pretty blue eyes; pretty dimples in her pink and white cheeks. She was a jolly little thing and men liked her. The young Minister of this narrative had come to the church as a bachelor and had hung around Sally for months until she (and possibly he, as well) decided that she was not the stuff of which ministers' wives are made. Then he had married a girl from his own home town, and Aunt Louisa had welcomed the bride with the most elegant evening party that Illyria had ever seen. She was nobody's fool, Aunt Louisa, and had no notion of letting it be rumored abroad that Sally had been jilted.

Sally didn't mind the Minister's defection. One day she stopped by the shoe factory, wearing her new flowery print tied back in a big loose bow, a flat disc of violets tipped over her impudent nose. And there in her father's office she met a new young man. He was a buyer from a wholesale house in the Capital come to do business with Uncle Warren, but after that meeting, his chief business was with Sally. Aunt Louisa disliked him from the first. "He is an ungodly man," she declared. He played cards for money; he drank; he belonged to no church. Even Uncle Warren didn't regard him highly.

But Sally, the small-town girl, was dazzled by the glamor of the Capital. He told her of life in the city; of the big hotels; and of dinners in smart restaurants. Calvinism had weighed heavily on Sally. Now she quietly slid from under. She didn't elope, nothing so dramatic as that. She just walked out one day and got married.

"I would rather see her dead and in her grave!" Aunt Louisa said with unwonted vehemence.

Divorces were almost unheard of in the South of those days. Public opinion was against them. Also, there was the Puritan assumption that people married for keeps, and that as ye make your bed so must ye lie on it. A divorced woman, whatever the rights of the case, was looked at askance. It was taken for granted that she would withdraw from life in a kind of social suttee.

But before so very long, here was Sally back again in her father's home, a divorced woman, and obviously not unduly upset. Certainly she staged no withdrawal. It is hard to say whether the divorce itself or Sally's nonchalant behavior was most distressing to her mother. "I am afraid that Sally is lacking in proper feeling," she said to Uncle Warren.

At this time marriage itself was to a certain extent a suttee. Again and again I have read in the society column of the Capital City's newspapers, a florid account of Miss So-and-So's wedding, which always ended with the remark, "Miss So-and-So has long been a leading Belle of the State, and she will be a great loss to society." The age of the Young Matron had not yet dawned!

However, the "Colonel's" wife, the lovely Meena, was on the way to upset that tradition. The "Colonel," much to his mother's concern, had reached the unconscionable age of twenty-eight without having been seriously interested in a girl. No doubt there was reason for his holding off. He had been very young when he attained success as a lawyer and the demands of his profession kept him busy. Moreover, he was the "strong silent man" of English fiction. A big man, like most of the men in our family, with Aunt Louisa's clear blue eyes, and a cool, remote way of looking at feminine beauty.

But when his time came, he *tumbled*. He met Meena, down from the North on a visit, and six weeks later they were married and established in a house midway between the Square and Uncle Warren's.

I never forgot my first sight of Meena. Aunt Louisa had assembled all the family connection, including the children, to welcome the bride, but the train, of course, was hours late and the small fry had to be carried off to bed in their own homes. Only I, being in residence, was allowed to take a nap on the sofa. I was awakened by a lovely, golden voice saying, "And this is little Margaret!" And there was Meena, all golden eyes and bronze hair, and wide laughing mouth. I thought her the most beautiful thing I had ever seen, and I still think I was right.

Elly Lou, too, was beautiful in her calm, serene way, but Meena was something different. If she came into a stodgy evening party, an electric current seemed to run through the room. People sat up and began to talk, to each other if they couldn't talk to Meena, and the party went with a bang.

She electrified Illyria. She was young, not much older than the students in our branch of the State University; she could sing and play almost any musical instrument; she could dance and act and paint enchanting portraits. All the lost aspirants for better things than the grubby little town furnished began to cluster around Meena. The women who in secret had read "French in the original" now openly formed a group to read the French classics. Meena assembled an orchestra which she herself directed. They wrote words and music, and produced operettas. One of them, I remember, dealt with the landing of Captain John

Smith at Jamestown, and Meena, with her beautiful bronze hair hidden by a streaming black wig, sang the role of Pocahontas. Decidedly Meena had not committed suttee when she married.

In addition to all her gifts, she was "smart," in the southern meaning of the word. When I suddenly turned pigeon-toed and was badgered with admonitions to "turn my toes out," and threatened with braces, Meena came back from the Capital with a pair of red shoes. Thereafter, vain thing that I was, my attention was centered on my feet and I had to walk properly to show off my red shoes.

She had no authority over me, of course, but she took it. If she discovered me working up a fine tantrum she carried me off to her house and put me in a room by myself. Not a dark room, and not locked, which would have sent me into a screaming rage, but a big, quiet, sunny room. "Think it over, my angel," she would say, "and tell me what you decide." And an hour or so afterwards, with my little jangled nerves rested and my little brain competently at work, I would emerge in the guise of the angel she had called me.

Once, many years later, Woodrow said, "When you suddenly stopped lying on the floor on your stomach, screaming by the hour, your Aunt Louisa hoped that you had been converted. Can you remember what really happened?"

I began to laugh. "Religion had nothing to do with it! Meena pointed out one day that other people didn't lie yelling on the floor. So I decided that it wasn't stylish."

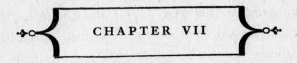

CHAPTER VII

AFTER BOTH the "Colonel" and Sally had married, and I was left alone in the house with Aunt Louisa and Uncle Warren, I might have felt terribly lonely had it not been for the servants, who after the fashion of the South of those days, were an integral part of the family.

Cindy, who had been a small girl at the time of the flight from the plantation, was now a woman in her late forties and, under Aunt Louisa, the working manager of the house. A colored boy Jake took her orders, and Luella her daughter, trained by Mammy Vina, reigned in the kitchen. Two men cared for the cows and horses and pigs and gardens. And Jim, Cindy's no-count husband, did odd jobs when he was out of jail. Once Jim demanded a dollar for a bit of carpentering he had done, and Uncle Warren gave him the devil.

"You ought to be ashamed of yourself," Uncle Warren

said. "Mis' Louisa gives you food and houseroom when you're free to enjoy it, and clothes you. And here you are asking for high wages when you ought to be glad to help her."

Jim scratched his shaved poll thoughtfully. "Now, Boss," he pleaded, "yo's got this all wrong. I does a lot o' wuk fo' Mis' Lou jes' out o' charity."

If Aunt Louisa's staff seems unreasonably extravagant, just remember the place and the times. The usual wage for a cook was five dollars—a *month*, not a week, and Meena's neighbors complained when she raised her old Mary, "a chef-cook" as the colored people called her, to six dollars. The food for the whole outfit must have cost very little. Poultry and eggs, vegetables and fruit all came from the place. After the autumn hog killing, hams and sides of bacon were hung in the smoke-house to cure. Tubs of creamy lard and pails of "cracklings" were lined up in the storeroom. On Uncle Warren's farm in the foothills, a mill turned by water power, supplied us and our friends with the water-ground corn meal so cherished by Southerners. If one of the cows gave birth to a bull calf, it was butchered and the meat shared with the neighbors. The domestic economy was almost self-sustaining.

I have little idea of the incomes of those days. Uncle Warren must have made a good profit from his shoe factory, but apparently money wasn't essential for comfortable living. The president of the bank in Illyria, on a salary of two thousand a year, brought up a family of four children. He had a good nine-room house, a horse in the stable and a cow in the barn, and was considered one of the "moneyed men" of the town.

In addition to Aunt Louisa's active staff (supposedly active!), there were Uncle Dan and Mammy Vina, now too old to work, living in the cabin which Uncle Warren had built for them out beyond the barn. I liked to drift by there in the late afternoon and see them sitting on their narrow porch, smoking their clay pipes, gazing out at the meadows beyond the pine woods. A picture of serene contentment. They had never minded the loss of the plantation, for to them Aunt Louisa spelled home.

They had both been famous singers in their day and even now, old and wrinkled and gnarled with rheumatism, they could hold their own with the young 'uns. When they grew too feeble to attend church, certain of the congregation used to gather at the cabin, and night after night we in the big house would hear those marvellous voices flinging their songs out into the darkness. If I could manage it, I always slid out after I had been sent to bed and hid in the bushes near the cabin.

They sang one spiritual which I never heard anywhere else—which, of course, does not mean that others did not sing it.

> *I'se a-comin' home* [they would chant]
> *I'se a-comin' home*
>
> *Good Lawd Gabr'l wid yo' golden horn*
> *Good Lawd Gabr'l wid yo' golden horn*
> *Blow lo-u-ud yo' golden horn.*
> *I'se a-comin' home,*
> *I'se a-comin' home.*

Good Lawd Peter at dem pearly gates,
Good Lawd Peter at dem pearly gates,
Open wi-i-de dem pearly gates,
I'se a-comin' home,
I'se a-comin' home.

Good Lawd God on yo' golden t'rone
Good Lawd God on yo' golden t'rone
Reach down fo' dis po' sinner, Lawd,
I'se a-comin' home,
I'se a-comin' home.

With the small night sounds in the bushes, and the darkness hedging me in, and the throb of those voices tearing at my heart, I felt delicious prickles go racing down my spine.

One evening, returning from one of these expeditions, I saw Woodrow leaning against a pillar of the upstairs porch, listening. It was natural enough that he should be there. Southerners have always enjoyed listening to negro spirituals, and Woodrow, although he hadn't a drop of southern blood in his veins, had been born in the South and reared in southern ways. He, too, had lived in little towns such as Illyria, and in his mother's house there must have been counterparts of our Cindy and old Dan and Mammy Vina, and after his long residence in the North, he must have been glad to hear "colored folks" singing. Moreover, he too was a singer, with a smooth tenor voice. During his undergraduate days he had sung on the Princeton Glee Club, and those harmonies coming to him out of the darkness must have delighted him.

But I knew nothing of all that. Glimpsing his dark figure leaning against the white column, I decided that he must be on the look-out for me. I drew back into the shadows unostentatiously and entered the house by way of the servants' porch and the kitchen, complacently sure that I had escaped detection. But next morning I discovered that Cindy knew all about it.

"I seed yo'-all hidin' behine them bushes down by Mam' Viny's cabin," she remarked, flipping a lavender scented sheet across my small bed. "Ef'n yo' don' quit this heah sneakin' out at night, I'll be bleeged to tell Mis' Lou."

"I wasn't doing any harm," I protested. "I was just listening. And Brother Woodrow was listening too. He was on the upstairs porch. I saw him."

"I seed him too." Cindy's clever black hands adjusted the counterpane smoothly. "Quality allus likes to hear us cullud folks sing. Maybe Mis' Elly Lou and Mister Woodrow does live way up nawth with them Yankees, but they ain't no nawthen trash. They's Quality, they is. 'Course he likes to hear us."

Quality! What is it? And why can negroes so unfailingly detect it?

Miss Henrietta Ricketts, Ellen's friend, once remarked: "If a hussy came to my house arrayed in velvet and furs, these Irish maids of mine would think her the real thing. But a negro can recognize quality even though it be hidden beneath rags."

My husband and I were selling our place outside Beverly Hills in California, and several motion picture

magnates came to look at it. One of them, a high-up director, took a fancy to our colored house boy, Rufus. I had
the story from the "realtor" who was showing the place.

Said the director: "If I buy the house, do I buy you with
it?"

The realtor said that Rufus looked the man straight in
the face and with exquisite courtesy and unrelenting firmness replied simply, "No, Sir!"

Rufus, too, told me about it afterwards. "He axed me
would he buy me ef'n he bought the house, and I said no,
Sir. But, Madame, what I wanted to say was, I wouldn't
work for no movie folks nohow. I likes to work for quality,
I does." (It is unnecessary, of course, to comment on
Rufus' unfairness in thus shoving the whole of a great in-
dustry into one pigeon hole.)

That story, I think, goes far to explain the extraordinary
devotion which the colored staff at the White House
showed to Woodrow. Like Cindy and her kind in Illyria,
they felt that the President was Quality, and they "liked
to work for quality." Those years in the White House were
tragic years for the Wilsons, first because of the heart-
breaking sorrow of Ellen's death, and then because of the
great world tragedy of the war. But notwithstanding the
tragedy, the White House was a pleasant place in those
days. Even a casual visitor sensed the atmosphere. The
colored servants felt that they "belonged" to the family,
and that the family belonged to them.

Later they proved their loyalty during Woodrow's
courtship of Mrs. Galt which, because of the restraint

placed on the movements of the President, of necessity took place within the White House itself. The servants, of course, knew what was happening. They saw Mrs. Galt arrive in a White House car with Helen; they saw the three walking in the garden; they served tea in the President's own study. But so far as anyone could learn, not one shred of gossip was ever put out by the staff. If questioned, and one or another of them was questioned frequently, he would assume the Sphinx-like look which his race can so easily assume, and smile blandly: "No Sir, there's nothing happening around heah that I know of!"

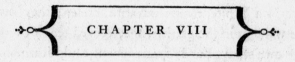
AS I BEGAN to dig into my memories of the Wilsons in my Aunt Louisa's house in Illyria, I was surprised to discover that it was chiefly Woodrow himself whom I glimpsed, and I wondered why that should be the case. The non-appearance of my nieces in these flash-backs is of course easily understood. They were younger, and Freddy and I were so busy hiding from them that they were probably pushed right out of the picture.

Elly Lou I do "see" very often. She was so pretty, and I liked to watch the sheen of her brown hair, her lovely soft brown eyes, and the shine of her white arms through black lace when she was dressed for a party. I admired her extravagantly, and no doubt she would have taken a far more important place in my memories had it not been for the fact that already there were two women dominant in the child Margaret's life. My Aunt Louisa, and Meena. Any other woman, even a queen on her throne, would have had hard work ousting those two from first place in my mind.

But there was no *man* in my circle who could rival Woodrow. Uncle Warren and the "Colonel" I adored, and for the other uncles and cousins who frequented the house, I felt varying degrees of affection. But—and in the last analysis it boils down to this—young as I was, I felt even then that "Brother Woodrow" was *different*. His not-too-frequent laughter delighted me; and that funny little twist of his lips when I said something that amused him; and the look of understanding in the gray eyes which I thought so attractive.

"A noticeable man." Thus Elly Lou had described him during their engagement. Had she so described him to me, I wouldn't have known what the *word* meant, but I fancy that I would have caught the deeper meaning. Even when their visits ended and the family left Illyria, I didn't forget my "Brother Woodrow."

Freddy, too, roughneck though he was, thoroughly approved of this visitor. "Gosh!" he would exclaim when we had chanced to meet Woodrow in our wanderings, "That's a regular guy!" and no doubt Freddy's approval helped to focus my attention on Woodrow.

During the months that followed Sally's marriage, Freddy and I were together almost constantly. Together we attended the dame's school of Miss Amanda McWhorter, and after school hours we had our diversions. A misguided friend gave Freddy a book of western stories, and taking that for a model we roped and tried to ride the three-months-old heifer. Old Rose, the mother, made short work of our rodeo. Changed in a flash from a well-behaved Jersey cow to the likeness of a raging bull in the arena, she came at us with lowered horns, bellowing her wrath, and Freddy and I fled ignominiously, tumbling over the barnyard fence just one inch ahead of death and destruction. Thoroughly scared for once, we looked at each other aghast, needing no words to pledge ourselves to silence.

But our next misdemeanor was so public that no concealment was possible. It happened one Sunday morning when Freddy, homeward bound from Mass, spied me standing outside our church while my Aunt Louisa spoke to an acquaintance. Now a few years before this time, an English lady had written a book which had brought anguish to thousands of American small boys. The Little Lord Fauntleroy craze was no doubt on the wane in the cities of the East, but in the provinces it was still rampant, and Freddy's mother had succumbed. Her son was a stocky young Irishman with a pug nose, and a wide mouth, and bristly red hair clipped as short as Freddy could persuade the barber to clip it. Nevertheless, his mother had made for him a suit of bright blue velvet, with a lace collar that hung down limply against his hefty chest.

This was my first sight of Freddy in his glory. My eyes bulged. "Goodness!" I exclaimed. "My goodness, but you're grand."

"Shut *up!*" Freddy snarled, clenching his fists beneath the blue velvet sleeves.

A whistle from up the street startled us. A group of Freddy's peers, likewise on their way home from Mass, had sighted him.

"Yah!" they shouted. "Mammy's little boy!" "Sissy!"

Freddy looked wildly down the street, then behind him to the open door of my church. He caught me by the arm. "Git in there quick!" he ordered. "I'm comin' with you."

Aunt Louisa found us sitting side by side in her pew. She glanced at Freddy in surprise, but far be it from her to object to anyone's presence in the house of the Lord. She sat down and leaning forward, rested her forehead against the back of the seat in front of her for a moment of silent prayer.

"Why don't she kneel down on the cushion?" Freddy demanded in a hoarse whisper, jabbing a grimy finger at Aunt Louisa's footstool.

"Hush!" I whispered back, unable to explain to him that Presbyterians didn't *kneel* in church.

Freddy managed well enough during what Presbyterians call the preliminary exercises. There was enough variety to interest him, but when we settled down to the business of the sermon he was done for. Sermons were *sermons* in those days; no mere quarter-hour discourse would have satisfied us. Freddy writhed and twisted and yawned. Finally he extracted a hymn book from the rack and a stub of a pencil from his blue velvet pocket and challenged me to a game of tit-tat-toe.

Even then all might have been well had we been content to play quietly, for Aunt Louisa, absorbed in her devotions, wasn't noticing. But this game, like most of our games ended in a riot. Thinking that I had caught him cheating, I seized a handful of lace collar and began to choke him. He retaliated, and we were so busy mauling each other that we didn't hear the break in the sermon's easy flow and were dragged back to our surroundings only when the Minister's voice, grave and troubled, publicly reproved us.

How he must have hated to do it, the poor young Minister, forced to rebuke the niece of his most valued parishioner! I rather fancy that in that moment Aunt Louisa's despair about me reached its nadir. That I, last of a long line of Puritans, should have been "spoken to" by the Minister from the pulpit. She sat throughout the rest of the service, more grim-faced than usual, and afterwards, dismissing Freddy with a word, she led me home to a dinnerless Sunday afternoon and an assignment of the Scripture that daunted even my quick-learning capacity.

The worst of it, in her opinion, was that I wouldn't *stay* chastened. I might howl at the flick of the peach switch, but five minutes afterwards she would hear me singing and laughing in the back yard. And the Monday after a dinnerless Sunday found me sleekly smiling at the breakfast table. Did she never suspect that Uncle Warren and Cindy saw to it that I didn't starve? And didn't she realize that, an exhibitionist of the front rank, I loved the drama of a row? That our day-in, day-out contests added zest to a boring existence? I don't know.

Besides Uncle Warren and Meena, there was another person with whom, however rambunctious I might feel, I refrained from staging rows—my brother Edward. He lived with Woodrow and Elly Lou in the North, but I saw him twice a year as he travelled to and from the military school in which Elly Lou had entered him.

Edward, so much older than I, might have been a bullying older brother, but he wasn't. He was firm with me, of course. Seeing me working myself up into a tantrum, he would fling me a casual glance. "Cut it out, youngster!" he would order. I cut it out. I did everything that he ordered. Had he told me to jump from the peak of the barn roof, I would have jumped without a backward glance, so anxious I was to win his approval. Those few days in autumn and summer when I had him were the high lights of my existence. Then one spring, the last before he was to go to college, an epidemic of measles closed his school, and Edward came to Aunt Louisa's.

I hadn't known he was coming. One morning, busied with spring planting in my flower bed below the porch, I heard the front gate click and, glancing up, I saw my brother. He was a handsome lad, tall and slim, vividly dark like his father—*oh, your dear dark head, darling, darling!* —and in his gold-buttoned uniform he looked to me a god. I gave a gasp of unbelieving rapture, then I whizzed down the brick walk like a bomb and exploded in his arms.

Long years have not dimmed the glory of that spring. Up and out of the house by sunrise, we made a preliminary tour of gardens and barns. Back for breakfast, then out again with a whole glorious day before us. He taught me to vault fences instead of prosaically climbing them; to shinny up the smooth trunk of a tree until I reached the first branches. Strapping the "Colonel's" boyhood saddle on to Sally's combination mare, he taught me to ride. "Learn on a cross-saddle," he decreed. "Then a side-saddle will be easy." I couldn't grip with my knees as he ordered for the simple reason that my legs wouldn't reach over the edges of the saddle, but I learned balance and control, and, once I became adept, our field of exploration was unlimited.

At this time I was supposed to be a pupil at Miss Amanda McWhorter's school, but Aunt Louisa, probably sensing that I would refuse to go anyway, decreed that I was to have a vacation this spring. So every morning when it wasn't raining—and, looking back, those mornings all seem to me golden—Edward and I were off, he mounted on Uncle Warren's gelding, our packets of lunch strapped to his saddle. Fortunate indeed is anyone who has one such spring to remember.

Aunt Louisa must have been, at bottom, a very understanding person. Years later, after my brother had died, I learned that she had written to Elly Lou: "It is a pity that young Edward cannot attend the college here. I think the child would like it."

The child would like it! A master of understatement, my Aunt Louisa!

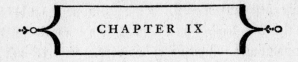

CHAPTER IX

ONE OF my Aunt Louisa's marked characteristics was her Puritan distrust of beauty. She loved her daughter-in-law Meena whole-heartedly but she never looked at that charming face without a twinge of fear. "You have a dangerous gift, daughter," she would say. That marked, perhaps, the fundamental difference between my aunt and me. I revelled in beauty, anybody's beauty, with a pagan abandon, and she was always trying to restrain me.

One morning I sat on my cousin Lulie's front steps waiting for Aunt Louisa, who was visiting with her daughter inside. I was wearing a new frock of pink dimity, my hair was tied back with a pink ribbon, and I felt rather more pleased with myself than usual. Two negro women walking past the house, stopped to look at me. "Lawdy!" one of them said. "Ain't she prutty!" I think it must have been my long straight hair that attracted them!

I was preening my feathers vaingloriously, when Aunt

Louisa appeared in the doorway. She had overheard the woman's remark and as we walked up the street, she delivered a sermon with the text "Pretty is as pretty does."

I listened in deepest discouragement. If good behavior were the measuring rod of beauty, then I was doomed to a life of ugliness. All at once, however, I cheered up. "But Aunt Louisa," I said, "Rosalie is *lovely* and she's not so awful good."

Rosalie, two or three years older than I, was my idea of a fairy princess. Eyes like blue pansies, peaches and cream complexion, shining golden curls floating down to her waist. I thought of those ringlets now and sighed. "I wouldn't mind *what* happened to me if I could have curls like Rosalie's," I said.

Aunt Louisa glanced down at my smooth brown head bobbing along beside her and the wistfulness in my voice must have gripped her heart. For the first, and only, time in her life Aunt Louisa abandoned her principles and paid me a compliment. "Ah, but Rosalie hasn't pretty brown eyes like yours," she said. It is a wonder that the words didn't choke her, so firm was her belief that to tell a child she was pretty would spoil her.

I looked up, radiant. "Oh, Aunt *Louisa!*" I breathed, and during the rest of our walk to the Square, I was dancing on air. *Aunt Louisa* had said that my eyes were pretty!

I loved our Square as an Italian loves his piazza. It was the center of my town. It was exciting. There was a bandstand up near the court house and on Saturday nights during the summer the Illyria band played there while people lounged on the dusty grass and listened. I had never been allowed to hear it, but I was still hopeful. This morning I looked at the lawyers sitting in split-bottomed chairs tilted against the walls of their one-storey offices, chatting and smoking, and, I am sorry to say, chewing tobacco. They all got to their feet as Aunt Louisa passed and lifted their hats. Two of them broke off a hot argument and bowed deeply. I liked it!

As we went on I asked Aunt Louisa what they were fussing about. She told me that most of those men had received excellent classical educations and spent their spare time reading Latin and discussing different passages. "Often they disagree," she remarked.

Just then the clerk of the court appeared at the top of the court house steps swinging a great dinner bell and chanting, "Oyez. Oyez. Oyez. The Honorable the Circuit Court is now in session. All ye who—" Then the lawyers dived into their offices and reappeared carrying green baize bags, and raced for the court house.

I watched it all enchanted. This was my town and I loved it: the friendly storekeepers waving a greeting to Miss Louisa's little girl; the pretty young ladies walking with their beaux; the horses and mules gnawing at the hitching rails in front of the stores. To me, unaware of its unkempt dilapidation, it was a happy town.

But that morning marked the end of my unawareness of tragedy. We had left Lulie, Aunt Louisa's beloved older daughter, alive and well, happily expecting a new baby. Two days later she was dead. The day after the funeral, I caught a glimpse of my aunt standing at the window of the room where her two little girls had slept as children. Something in that black gowned, starkly rigid figure frightened me, and I began to sob. "God is mean to kill Lulie," I wept. "I hate him!"

Aunt Louisa looked at me with hot, dry, tearless eyes. "Hush, child!" she ordered. "The ways of Providence are inscrutable. Though He slay me, yet will I trust Him."

It was after this that she began to withdraw into herself. It was more than a physical withdrawing, for the town and Aunt Louisa had come to a parting of the ways. They were no longer in sympathy. Her spiritual home was war and depressions, hard times that tried men's souls and demanded every ounce of strength from their bodies. She wasn't geared to easy living and prosperity. How she would have hated our nineteen twenties, and how well adjusted she would be to the days in which we are now living.

The years had passed swiftly and Illyria had emerged from a boom period into settled prosperity. New factories had been built; the streets of factory workers had grown longer (and dingier). The few fine old houses that had survived Sherman's passing were torn down, and turretted, balconied atrocities had arisen in their place. Some of these new houses, we boasted, had two bathrooms apiece.

But if modern sanitation had reached indoors, in the town itself it was still non-existent. Every Monday morning the gutters ran blue with the water from a thousand wash tubs—a phenomenon to be seen in the great city of Baltimore long after it had vanished from Illyria. The unpaved streets, ankle-deep with red dust in the summer, turned to quagmires of ochre mud in the winter. Huge stepping stones laid from sidewalk to sidewalk were supposed to afford safe passage to pedestrians. A vain delusion. For the stones were smooth and slick, the mud between them bottomless. Small boys in rubber boots earned many an honest penny by arming themselves with two boards and leading timid women across that perilous bridge of sighs.

One morning as I drifted down our street, I came upon Freddy escorting our school teacher Miss Amanda across the slough. At the moment of my arrival, Miss Amanda— round and fat, with feet too tiny to be useful—was teetering in midstream waiting for Freddy to clamp his second board into position. Now I liked Miss Amanda. Moreover I had long been fretted by Freddy's access to this unlimited source of income. Ignoring the fact that I was bootless, I plunged in, and seized the free end of the board.

The result was foreordained. While Freddy and I fought grimly for possession of the board, Miss Amanda slid off the rounded stone and plunged into the red mud with a splash and a squawk of outraged dignity.

"This settles it!" Freddy's father exclaimed when he learned of the incident. "The girl is ruining the lad. I'll send him to the priests' school in Kentucky."

The Jesuits say that if they can have a boy through his sixth year, they care not who has him afterwards. I had had Freddy for much longer than six years. I wonder what the priests made of him—afterwards!

Aunt Louisa's blue eyes darkened when I told her why

Freddy was being sent away. "The injustice of it!" she remarked. She would engage in no neighborhood feud, but after that her relations with Freddy's parents became strictly formal and in the autumn, instead of returning to Miss Amanda's school, I was entered at the Susie Carter Seminary for Young Ladies.

This was one of the two educational institutions of which Illyria boasted, the other being the branch of the State University. Every afternoon the young bloods of the College promenaded up and down in front of the Seminary, hoping for a glimpse of the sirens hidden behind those brick walls. Young and uninitiated, I knew nothing of the secret communications that passed between them, and when the older girls welcomed me with open arms, I accepted it smugly as an only-to-be-expected tribute to my charms.

But Meena, the "Colonel's" wife, knew better. "Listen, Margaret," she said crisply, "in no circumstances are you to carry notes from the girls to the College students whom you meet in my house."

I understood then, and my conceit flopped badly. Meena was musical; she was gay and beautiful; the "Colonel" himself was a perfect host. It was no wonder that the most attractive young men in the college flocked to their house. And the girls cloistered in the Seminary knew of that flocking. They looked at me with envy. That I, a slip of a thing with my hair bound back like Alice in Wonderland, should have free access to those gatherings, while they themselves were barred! Even when I told them that I couldn't serve as messenger, they continued to cultivate me, no doubt hoping that some chance word of mine would direct the boys' thoughts in their direction. Little by little the older girls who lived in the town began inviting me to their parties.

And with those invitations came new complications, for Aunt Louisa was fundamentally, unbudgingly, fanatically opposed to dancing. To her it was more than a venial sin. Women who danced and men who gambled were bracketed in her mind. Sober-minded Lulie had shared her mother's opinion. Sally, the pleasure loving, had evaded the issue by going docilely up to bed and then slipping down the outside stairs of the back gallery to join her friends at a party. Even the "Colonel" as a stripling had had his own exits and entrances.

Had Aunt Louisa learned of her children's exploits and realized belatedly that Puritanism often begets deceit in in the non-Puritan? I don't know. Certain it is that something had changed her. She might well have made me refuse those invitations on the ground of my extreme youth, but she didn't even suggest it. Only—"I want you to promise me not to dance," she said almost mildly.

At that my small red mouth closed in what must have been a ludicrous replica of her own. "But I've just got to dance, Aunt Louisa," I declared. "I've just *got* to. When I see the other girls dancing my feet sort of itch."

I never forgot the look she gave me. At that moment, probably, she realized her defeat. I was a Calvinist child, sprung from an appalling array of Presbyterian ministers. Unquestionably I was predestined to *something*. But not—

as Aunt Louisa now recognized—not to be a shining light of the church.

She made one last effort at control when she spied a jewelled badge pinned to the collar of my blue sailor blouse. "What is that?" she demanded.

I launched into excited explanations. It was Charles' fraternity pin and Charles was the newest College hero. "You know, a boy gives you his pin and then you're his girl. All the other girls were sick when he gave it to me."

Aunt Louisa was not impressed. "At your age!" she commented.

But Uncle Warren's Baptist eyes twinkled. "It's predestination, or something, Mis' Louisa! You might as well give up."

She glanced down at us coldly. "You will return the pin today, or I will return it tomorrow."

Yes, it really was a miracle that I didn't hate my Aunt Louisa.

Charles was waiting for me at his accustomed corner. Weeping, I thrust the pin into his hand. "She says, Aunt Louisa says, that I can't keep it. She says I'm not old enough to be thinking about boys," I wailed.

Charles looked at me. I had just entered my teens, but beneath my floppy hat, my tear-stained face still showed childishly round; my hair still hung down my back in a straight brown mane. "I think maybe she's right," he said thoughtfully. His eyes brightened suddenly. "I'll tell you what we'll do. *I'll* wear the pin and every time you look at it, you'll know you're my girl, and you'll promise not to wear anybody else's pin until you're old enough to wear mine."

This was the real thing! This was high romance! I thought of my rivals' faces when they heard of our pact. "Oh, Charles," I bubbled happily. "Oh *Charles!*"

Aunt Louisa knew that she had won only an empty victory. She could handle Calvinism and a conviction of sin, but a child who didn't recognize sin when she met it was beyond her. Perhaps that was why they decided that, when the autumn came, I should go north to school.

Several years had passed since Elly Lou and Woodrow had visited Illyria. He had become more and more distinguished in his profession, going from his first post in Bryn Mawr to Wesleyan College in Connecticut and finally to Princeton, his own college. For him these years had been extraordinarily productive. His *Congressional Government*, the thesis for his degree, had been followed by *The State*, by his *George Washington*, and by several volumes of essays. Now he was working on his history of the American people. No wonder that he no longer had time for visiting his relatives.

Yet Elly Lou didn't want to lose touch with her small sister. Also both she and Woodrow had decided that I needed more education than the Seminary for Young Ladies was giving me. So the decision was made, and on a shining June day I left Illyria behind me.

The town seemed strangely unaware of the significance of the occasion. The horses tethered along the Square gnawed unconcernedly at their wooden hitching posts.

Outside the one-storey offices, the lawyers still sat in their split-bottomed chairs and discussed the coming election. At the station a lanky negro shoved my trunk into the baggage car and turned away whistling. Didn't he know, didn't he *realize*, that I was leaving forever?

The family had come down to see me off, and a few girls from the Seminary, and at the last minute yellow-haired Charles came loping down the platform with a gaily wrapped package in his hand. I knew at once what it was— a five-pound box of candy, my first, my very first from a boy. I seized it ecstatically. "Oh Charles!" I whispered.

"Don't make yourself sick eating candy on the train," warned Aunt Louisa.

The teacher with whom I was travelling was already in the car. The conductor called all aboard. There was a wild rush of kisses liberally bedaubed with tears. The train began to move. From the car platform I waved frantically. Good-bye, Charles. Good-bye, darling Uncle Warren. Then suddenly that erect black figure motionless on the edge of the crowd, caught at my heart. I flung out my arms in a wide gesture—"It's good-bye, but only for now. Good-bye, Aunt Louisa!"

PART III

-›o‹-

The House of In-Laws
Library Place

CHAPTER X

WHEN I reached Princeton on that long ago June day, I found that my sister was no longer Elly Lou. She was Ellen.

"Aunt Louisa won't like that," I plucked up courage to warn. "Cousin Mary Lou wants us to call her just Mary, and Cousin Fanny Lou is plain Fanny, and it hurts Aunt Louisa's feelings."

Deep down in my subconsciousness I felt that my Aunt Louisa was entitled to this one tiny vanity, her only one. I knew that she had liked having her nieces named for her. It had seemed proof of the enduring affection of her brothers. And now the wretched nieces were betraying her. If only Elly Lou *wouldn't!* But my sister smiled her lovely, vague smile, and said nothing.

I turned away disheartened. Oh well, it was just one more strange thing in this strange new town. Dinner at night, for instance, and *white* women to wait on me. When

Annie, the second maid, offered to help me with my bath, I turned scarlet, said no thank you, firmly, and locked the bathroom door behind her.

The first few days hadn't been bad, for my brother Edward was there to give me a feeling of home. But now, a budding chemist, he had gone to a summer job in the Edison laboratories. I missed him. I missed my meanderings in fields and woods with Freddy. The sedate walks down the street with my nieces seemed tame. There was too much dress-up about those walks; the houses behind clipped hedges or low stone walls were too appallingly neat. I thought regretfully of Illyria's white picket fences—with many of the pickets missing—along which I had drawn my hoop stick with a gratifying clatter.

In the Wilsons' back yard—or rather, in their garden, for there were no back yards in Princeton—stood a magnificent copper beech. I had heard Elly Lou (I mean *Ellen*) remark that they had bought the lot because of that tree. I wasn't surprised. It was a glorious tree, with huge limbs spaced just right for climbing. One day, a week after my arrival, I persuaded my nieces to climb it.

Two of them stuck on the first limb; the third reached the second. I went on and up. It was almost too easy to be exciting. Two thirds of the way to the top, I came upon my brother's initials cut deep in the smooth bark. I straddled the out-jutting branch and ran my fingers over the letters. E.W.A., Edward William Axson. I could have climbed farther, of course, but I didn't. As high as he had gone was high enough for me.

I heard Annie's voice calling, heard my nieces' reply and the sound of their footsteps hurrying back to the house. My nieces puzzled me, they were so different from my friend Nell Murphy back in Illyria, and from Freddy and me. Their frocks were always miraculously tidy, and it never seemed to occur to them to disobey an order. What bewildered me most, however, was their way of lumping themselves together. "Marga-Jessie is going to bed," they would say. Or, "Jessie-Marga has a new dress." Only the littlest one, Nell, had managed to emerge from the ruck.

I slid down from my high perch—it was almost like walking down stairs—and dropped to the leaf-strewn ground. Beyond me only a few feet distant was the study, and I saw Woodrow seated by the open window. He was writing and I could see his hand moving smoothly across the paper. His face with the big nose and long jaw stood out sharply against the shadowy room behind him. Just so I had seen him often, seated at the pine table beneath my Aunt Louisa's oak tree. I felt a sudden lump in my throat.

Woodrow glanced up, saw me standing there watching him. Something forlorn in my appearance must have struck him, for into his suddenly narrowed eyes there came a gleam, a flash of light that seemed to prick out all my small, hidden misery. He rested one hand on the window-sill and leaned out.

"It's rather different from Illyria, isn't it? he said companionably.

I nodded dumbly. I had passed my thirteenth birthday,

but in many ways I was young for my age, and these child-ish fits of shyness still hit me at inconvenient times. Wood-row smiled.

"You'll grow accustomed to it after a bit. Don't worry."

He turned back to his writing, and I moved off slowly toward the house. The lump in my throat had dropped lower. It was now pressing, hard as a rock, against what I fancied was my heart. A horrible thought struck me. A pain in my heart. *Heart disease!* People died of pains in the heart. I looked frantically around me. The June sunshine lay golden on the thick, green grass, so different from Illyria's patchy lawns, and I realized suddenly that this place was beautiful, that I liked it. I didn't want to die and leave it.

I dragged myself upstairs to my room, almost paralyzed with terror at the thought of death. At home, in Illyria, when people were dying, the Minister read the Bible to them. There was no minister here, but my Aunt Louisa had packed my Bible (the one I had earned for reciting the Shorter Catechism) into my trunk and had made me promise to read a "portion" every night. I took it from the shelf and crouched down on the floor by the window. Now it came to me of a sudden that my Aunt Louisa had done me a great disservice in making me learn so much of the Bible by heart. Verse after verse about death came leaping into my mind. *This night thy soul shall be required of thee.* (This night, this very night!) *Prepare to meet thy God, O Israel.*

Well, I was preparing, wasn't I? I breathed out what was probably the first real prayer of my life. "Please God, don't make me die to-night!" Resolutely I opened the Bible and began to read.

An hour later Ellen found me, slumped down on the floor, fast asleep. I opened my eyes groggily when she spoke to me. At first I was so glad to find myself still alive that I ignored my strange sick feelings. But Ellen noticed my flushed face.

"Why, my dear, I believe you have fever!" she exclaimed, and the thermometer which she fetched from her medicine cabinet proved her right. Before she had me tucked into bed, I was shivering.

"Malaria" the doctor whom she summoned pronounced it, but *I* called it chills-and-fever. The doctor said I had brought it with me from the South, but I put the blame on Princeton. Ellen hadn't given me the large doses of quinine with which my Aunt Louisa always anticipated the dangerous season.

Woodrow and my nieces looked in on me. "I thought this afternoon that something was wrong," Woodrow remarked, smiling down at me.

I had always liked his smile, even back in those Illyria days which now seemed so far distant. It was such a gray-eyed, friendly smile. Now, even in my misery, it brought me a ray of comfort. He had smiled in just that way at my Aunt Louisa. All at once I knew that as long as Woodrow was around, I wouldn't be entirely cut off from my Aunt Louisa and home.

The malaria ran its course. I lay there, alternately burning and shivering, completely miserable. The truth was, I had probably been badly spoiled, in spite of Aunt Louisa's stern discipline. I had been the only child in a household of grown-ups, white and colored. All their interest had been centered on me. Here I found myself just one of four little girls, and I was nobody's center of interest. The house itself seemed strange to me, accustomed as I was to Aunt Louisa's big, cool, high-ceilinged, *empty* rooms. Here, I was conscious always of the presence of unseen people. I heard their footsteps on the stairs, their voices in the hall. They popped into my room, popped out again. I was desperately lonely, but also I was oppressed by the feeling of too-many-people.

Even now Woodrow did not fail me. His father, old Dr. Joseph Wilson, had arrived the day after I fell ill, and he demanded most of his son's leisure. But Woodrow managed to see me once or twice a day. He would come in cheerfully but not *too* cheerfully, always with some ridiculous story to tell me. One was about a man suffering with chills-and-fever, as I was. One day he was about to drink a glass of milk when the chills struck him, and the shivering churned the milk into butter. Woodrow acted it out for my amusement, shuddering along every inch of his well-poised, supple body.

I grew better and was allowed to sit in an easy chair by the window. My little room was over the front door, and now I could see the family's out-goings and in-comings. I still thought there were an awful lot of people crowded into one house. Woodrow and Ellen and the three girls, Maggie the cook and Annie the second maid, old Dr. Wilson, and Woodrow's sister Mrs. Howe and her daughter Little Annie, who had stopped off for a few days on their way south. My brother Stockton Axson was spending the summer in the rooms of a professor friend down on Nassau Street, and he rode up on his bicycle every day for lunch or dinner with the family.

In the Illyria of my time, grown men seldom rode bicycles. It was a horsey town, and if the men didn't ride horseback or drive in their buggies they walked. But here in Princeton bicycles seemed the only means of getting around. From my window I could see tall, severe-looking Professor Harry Fine, who lived opposite, pedalling sedately down the street, and Woodrow's classmate Professor Billy Magie, equally tall but less sedate. Stockton's method of riding tickled me. He sat reared far back in the saddle, and handled the bicycle gingerly as though fearful that the thing might buck. Woodrow, of course, managed it competently. He would snap the metal clips about his trousers, step on the pedal, and be off, not too fast and not too slowly, with the clean precision that characterized all his movements.

I was horribly bored by my convalescence, and I looked around for amusement. My nieces, who were even younger for their ages than I was, were still thrilled by the Red and Blue Fairy Books which I, accustomed to life more in the raw, found dull. Then, one day, it occurred to me that we could *act* these stories. At first, remembering Meena in the role of Pocahontas, I thought we might *sing* them, but since only one of us, Marga, could carry a tune, that project had to be abandoned. As author, producer and stage manager combined, I had things pretty much my own way, the protests of the others availing nothing. In Jessie, with her long pale gold hair and her beauty, I had the perfect fairy princess. Nell, already showing the dash and verve which later distinguished her, was the third of the three adventuring brothers, the one who carried off the prize. For audience we had Ellen and Annie the maid, long-suffering victims.

Maggie the cook would have none of us. "Indade, and I'm too busy cooking your dinners to be bothering wid your play-acting," she announced firmly. And Woodrow when approached, was equally firm.

"Indade, and I'm too busy earning the money to buy the food for Maggie to cook, to be bothering wid your play-acting," he declared.

Wise man! He loved his three little daughters and was fond of his small sister-in-law, but he would *not* watch their play-acting.

The summer drew to a close and my brother Edward came back. I was shortly to go off to school, and he to Massachusetts Tech for graduate work in chemistry, but we had a few weeks together, and we spent them exploring the countryside. There were no saddle horses here, of course, but with part of his earnings at the Edison laboratories, Edward bought me a fine new bicycle, and morning after morning we started out with lunches provided by

Maggie tied to our handle bars. Sometimes we would cache our bicycles under a hedge and take to the woods on foot.

On one such occasion, I seemed to glimpse the fleeting glory of these expeditions and all at once I went mad. I climbed trees and jumped from their lowest branches into my brother's arms; I scrambled over barbed wire fences, indifferent to the jagged tears in my skirt; finally I went hip-hopping down a hill yelling like a Comanche Indian. At the foot of the hill was a small stream, a tame little stream compared to our noisy southern rivers, but it drew me like a magnet. I plunged in, slipped on a smooth stone and sat down suddenly.

Someone laughed aloud. Getting to my feet, drenched, my torn skirt flapping about my bare brown legs in sopping tatters, I saw on the opposite bank of the stream a young man, one of the, to me, god-like race of "college students."

"Hi, Eddie," the young man called, and "Hi, Eddie," replied my brother.

Terribly embarrassed, I tried to hide behind my brother, but he dragged me forward, and introduced me.

"I've heard of you," the young man said. "Andy, my roommate, asked if I'd seen Ed Axson's kid sister and told me I'd better take a look at her." The eyes of the two Edwards met above my touselled head. "I'm taking it now!" the young man added.

Edward told about it that evening at dinner. "Taking a look or taking the girl?" Woodrow queried.

"Why, Brother Woodrow," I hooted, "he *couldn't* take *me!*"

"Couldn't he? Stranger things have happened," Woodrow observed.

Stranger things did happen. Some time afterwards a scholarship was offered which would give the recipient two years in a German university. Woodrow himself was to choose the lucky man. He had the rare gift of remembering the students who had done good work with him, and now he thought of that second Edward.

"What's become of that chap who took all my courses in government, and then switched over to classics?" he asked.

"He's teaching Latin in the School of Science," my brother Edward replied.

Now Woodrow was a fairly good classical scholar himself, but his real love was government, theory of the state, jurisprudence, and to have a man who had been one of his best students abandon that field for Latin was anathema. "We must get him out of that," he remarked.

So the young man went to Heidelberg and returned with his Ph. D. degree to be Woodrow Wilson's assistant. By that time I was "grown-up," and—"I raised that child to be my wife," the second Edward insisted.

To which Woodrow would always retort, "And I educated *you* to be her husband."

But all that was still far in the future. Now at the tail end of my first Princeton summer, I was still too young and too absorbed in my brother to give a thought to any other boy—not even to the vanished Freddy or to Charles whose fraternity pin I had promised to wear when I reached years of discretion. Edward and I could wander through the meadows and woods all day, but in the evening he had typing to do for Woodrow, and I would establish myself on the window-seat close by his typewriter table. Occasionally Woodrow would come in, consult with Edward about the manuscript for a few minutes, and then fling me a smile as he went out.

Even then I was vaguely aware of his sympathetic understanding of the relationship between my brother and me. I felt that, unobtrusively, he was making it possible for us to be constantly together. Years later I realized the reason for that sympathy. He told me of his own older sister, who, next to his father, had been his most cherished companion. She must have had a mental equipment comparable to Woodrow's own. In the years after the Civil War, when money was so scarce, she had earned many an honest penny by translating foreign manuscripts for a Boston publishing house. And that, for a young southern girl of that period, was no mean achievement. Then she married and went farther west to live, and then died.

"She had meant a great deal to me," Woodrow said. "Of all human relationships, that of brother and sister is one of the most perfect, when it is perfect. Born of the same stock, they are alike, yet born man and woman, they are sufficiently unlike to find each other interesting."

The summer ended at last. I had hated the sissy neatness of clothes which Ellen demanded. I had missed my freedom; and the barnyard full of animals that were always giving birth to new babies; and the negro servants who handled me with adoring firmness, training me in what they considered proper manners. ("A little lady don't act like that, honey," Cindy would say.) But somehow I had managed to adjust myself without too much friction. And then, just before Edward and I departed for our respective educational institutions, another strange thing happened. A governess for my nieces arrived, imported from Germany.

Edward met her at the station and they reached the house shortly before luncheon. One by one her future pupils were presented to her. She looked them over carefully, then looked at me, standing a little apart. "And dis one, who is dis?" she demanded, evidently suspecting that one more pupil than she had bargained for was to be run in on her.

"You won't have anything to do with me," I said promptly. "I'm going off to school." And I added under my breath, "Thank goodness!" For I didn't like the look of her pale, fishy eyes.

"Ach!" Fräulein Clara snorted.

She turned briskly to Ellen. "Und now I vould like to vash my hands before ve eat."

She bustled out of the room escorted by Marga. Woodrow's eyes followed her. "Poor thing," he said, with a shade of doubt in his voice. "She must be feeling very far away from her home."

It seems strange that a youngish professor could afford the luxury of a governess, but there was no girls' school in Princeton at that time, and I suppose Woodrow and Ellen decided that it would be cheaper to import a governess than to pay fees for three daughters at a good boarding school. I suppose, too, that it was natural they should choose a German rather than a French woman. The leading writers of the day in Woodrow's field were German, and Ellen had long read widely in the German philosophers.

At any rate, whatever the reason, Fräulein Clara came and for years was an uncomfortable addition to the household. Her father had been a professor in a Prussian university and Fräulein was the embodiment of Prussianism. From her first coming she took a dislike to Marga, and the years resolved themselves into a running battle between them. She bullied the poor girl unmercifully.

"You have the hands of a peasant," she would say, though it wasn't in the least true. "Look at your hands and then look at Jessie's. Ach! How did the daughter of your mother acquire such hands!" Brutal stuff to hand out to a girl who already labored under the disadvantage of having an exquisitely beautiful younger sister.

The girls should have told their parents of course. Or I should have. But it never occurred to any of us. They were obedient young things and, having been put under the authority of a governess, I suppose they thought that it was their duty to submit. As for me, I found it hard to believe that anyone could take the woman seriously enough to be made unhappy by her. I saw her only during my holidays from school when she insisted upon talking to me in French. With the result that no Frenchman has ever been able to understand one word that I utter!

She made no attempt to adapt herself to the ways of

the household. "In my country," she would say through narrowed lips. "In *my* country we do things differently."

On one occasion she was holding forth to her pupils on the glory and power of the Prussians, past and future. Nell listened with wide apprehensive eyes. "But Fräulein," she gasped, "if Prussia and America went to war, you wouldn't hurt *us*, would you?"

The woman's eyes hardened. "If mein Kaiser ordered me to kill you, I vould do it at once—like this—" and she drew a finger across her throat with an ugly gesture.

Nell, poor child, began to sob, and appeared at luncheon sodden with tears. She wouldn't tell what had happened. But long after the house had been mercifully relieved of Fräulein's presence, I happened to mention the incident to Woodrow. He said nothing but his eyes grew dark with anger. Yes, that was one occasion when I saw Woodrow Wilson really angry!

CHAPTER XI

THAT FIRST summer in Princeton left three impressions deeply engraved in my brain. The first, of course, was of my brother Edward. I always thought of him first when I thought of my family. The second was of Woodrow's understanding of my misery during those early days. I couldn't have put it into words. As a matter of fact, it never reached the form of definite thought. But deep down inside me I knew that after this Woodrow would be to me more than just my brother-in-law; he would be a friend. The third impression was of a house as brimful of people as a coffee cup with coffee.

At my Aunt Louisa's there had always been nieces and nephews and cousins coming and going, but somehow the big, sprawling old house with its cool, lofty rooms had seemed to absorb them with no disruption of itself. It had a personality of its own that no intrusion from outside could upset . The cousins came, fell at once into the pattern, and I, at least, could forget them. In the Princeton house, on the contrary, the outsiders seemed always under foot. No wonder that, later, I was to think of the place as the House of In-laws.

Did either Woodrow or Ellen, I wonder, ever count up the number of days when they were alone in their house? There must have been precious few. When Woodrow was a professor in Bryn Mawr, Ellen's young brother Edward Axson, lived with them. At Wesleyan College in Middletown, Connecticut, they had with them in addition to Edward, Ellen's older brother Stockton Axson, and Woodrow's brother Joe Wilson, both of them students at the College. At Princeton they had Woodrow's father, his sister Mrs. Howe, her daughter little Annie, and her son George Howe, a classmate of Edward's. The two boys roomed on the campus but for their first two years took their meals with the Wilsons. Helen Bones, Woodrow's beautiful young cousin, was a resident member of the household only after they went to the White House, but during her boarding school days, she spent her week-ends in the Library Place house. And now I was added to the heterogeneous collection!

In the spring before my coming, the Wilsons had moved from the house long known as "Granny Hunt's" into the English type, stone and stucco house which they had built next door, on the lot dominated by the copper beech tree. Ellen's friend, Miss Henrietta Ricketts, owns it now and complains that there are too many bedrooms. Well, Woodrow and Ellen needed a lot of bedrooms!

Of course all this horde of in-laws was never on hand at the same time. Not even the Wilsons could have stood that. But they came and went. Old Dr. Wilson up from the South or down from Saratoga, his favorite Spa. Mrs. Howe and Annie from their impermanent perches in South Carolina or New York or Philadelphia. George Howe, and Stockton and Edward Axson appearing regularly or irregularly for meals. I myself bobbing up from school and college and years abroad. We might wander here and there over the country, but for me, as for the others in that curiously flitting crowd, Woodrow's house was the place to which we always returned.

As I look back, the strangest thing about the whole layout was that no one of us thought it strange, least of all Woodrow and Ellen. We were all Southerners of course, which perhaps explains it. We had been reared in the southern tradition of prolonged and intensive hospitality when a cousin might come for a week's visit and remain for the rest of her life. Also we were accustomed to the southern feeling of responsibility for the unattached members of the clan. Ellen felt responsible for her little sister and her two younger brothers. Woodrow's home had been broken up after his mother's death, and it was only to be expected that his father should turn to his favorite son for companionship. It wasn't a question of money that made us turn to Princeton, for all of us had something to scrabble along with. But no one of us had a home, and to Woodrow and Ellen we owed the feeling that somewhere on the earth's surface there was a house we could call home.

I can look back from this distance and see Woodrow, so friendly and courteous and considerate, seated at the head of his long dining table, flanked by two rows of his own and Ellen's relatives. Did he ever wonder why, in addition to a man's normal responsibilities, fate should have wished onto him this unending stream of in-laws? If that thought did come to him occasionally, he certainly managed to hide it.

It must have taken a lot of managing to fit us all in, and Ellen of course had to do it; yet in all those years I heard from her only two complaints—first, that her maids had to be constantly airing and de-mothing the furs we left in her attic, and next, that we were all provokingly casual.in announcing our times of arrival.

"Won't you at least let me know the *day?*" she would beg. But that request always brought a storm of protest, even from her own daughters. "But Mother, we don't always *know!*" "But Sister, I might want to accept a last-minute invitation!"

Ellen had been a dreamy, impractical girl, and when certain family friends heard of her engagement to Woodrow they predicted for him the horrors of a badly run house. Perhaps that prediction frightened the young bride. Anyway, as soon as she was established in Bryn Mawr, she went in to Philadelphia and arranged for lessons with Mrs. Rorer, the domestic science expert of her day. From her Ellen learned household management from the ground up. She knew how to train her servants. Better still, she knew how to keep them. Maggie the cook came when Nell was a baby and remained until we four girls were young ladies. Annie the second girl stayed until she married. Thus it was that Ellen, buttressed by her acquired practicality and by her two faithful maids, could face undismayed the thousand and one problems of the in-laws.

Again looking back from today, I am appalled at thought of the vast amount of food which all the in-laws must have consumed. So far as I know none of us ever paid a cent for board and lodging. Certainly I didn't. Even when I grew older it never occurred to me to offer to pay, and I am quite certain that it never occurred to Woodrow and Ellen. As I have said, all of us had grown up in the South where unlimited hospitality was the rule, not the exception.

Ellen had trained herself to be a good manager. She knew how to cut corners and to save, but even so the food had to be paid for, and their generous hospitality must have cost them many little luxuries and outings which they would have otherwise enjoyed. Of course the purchasing power of the dollar was at least double what it is today, but that doesn't detract from one's appreciation of the Wilsons' generosity.

Woodrow held the McCormick Professorship of Jurisprudence, a chair established for him and one of the best endowed professorships in the academic world of that time. For six weeks of every year, for many years, he delivered a course of lectures at Johns Hopkins University for which he received adequate fees. His books were now bringing in satisfactory royalties, two of them, *The State*, and *Division and Reunion,* being standard textbooks in the colleges. He was more and more in demand as a public speaker, and the higher-class magazines were glad to accept his articles. Moreover Ellen had (as had I) a modest patrimony from our father and grandfather Axson—the latter having been that *rara avis,* a well-to-do Presbyterian minister.

So taken by and large, the Wilsons with their young daughters were better off than the average professor of those days—if it hadn't been for those darned in-laws! (The above ejaculation is mine, not Woodrow's or Ellen's.)

One curious thing about the House of In-laws was that no one seemed to know, or care, which in-law belonged to whom. Ellen loved Woodrow's beautiful young cousin Helen Bones better than any of her own cousins, and when she went to the White House she took Helen with her as personal secretary and companion. Young as I was, Woodrow undoubtedly found me more companionable than he did his own sister, Mrs. Howe. Of Ellen's two brothers, the younger, Edward, in large measure took the place of the son Woodrow would have liked to have, and Stockton Axson, the older, was Woodrow's closest friend as long as they both lived. The two were very different in temperament, Woodrow being the stronger and more sharply disciplined, but there was enormous sympathy between them, and in so far as an outsider could judge, there was never the shadow of a cloud to dim the light of their friendship.

Woodrow dedicated all of his books to Ellen with the exception of *An Old Master* which he inscribed to his friend and classmate Robert Bridges, and *Mere Literature,* on the fly leaf of which is this inscription—"To Stockton Axson, by every gift of mind, a critic and lover of letters; by every gift of heart, a friend, this volume is affectionately dedicated."

Ellen herself long afterwards took her copy of the book from the shelf and showed me the inscription. As she did it, her lovely dark eyes shone happily. "It is a wonderful thing," she said, "when one's husband and brother are such friends. And also," she added, "what Woodrow says is so beautiful."

It was more than beautiful—it was *true*. More than anyone I have ever known Stockton had the divine gift of friendship. Nature had apparently planned him to that end. At the time of which I am writing he was still in his early thirties, good-looking, although not *handsome* as was his brother Edward, of a lean, hollow-jawed, "that-man-must-be-interesting" type. Woodrow always declared that Stockton must have been the model for Sargent's painting of the Prophet Hosea in the Boston Public Library, and one day to prove his contention, he took a white cashmere shawl of Ellen's and draped it over Stockton's head and shoulders, *à la* the Prophet. The likeness really was striking.

Later, unfortunately, Stockton lost the Hosea look. The lean jaws plumped out, and his rather angular body grew stout. But he never lost one thing with which nature had endowed him, a voice that could have charmed the birds out of the skies, and *did* charm men and women alike. How much of his enormous success as a lecturer in English literature was due to this golden voice, no one can say.

Undoubtedly it was an asset of great value. But he had more than a voice. As Woodrow had written, he was "by every gift of mind, a critic and lover of letters." He had also a strain of deep spirituality, not definitely expressed perhaps but permeating his lectures. As a friend of his put it, "Stockton is really one of his Presbyterian preacher ancestors who happened to get side-tracked."

I remembered this remark one summer after my husband and I had moved to California and Stockton was lecturing in the Greek Theatre at the University of California in Berkeley. Several of my San Francisco friends crossed the Bay every morning to attend his lectures, commiserating with me because Stockton's phobia against any of his family in the audience prevented my accompanying them.

One of these women, a gayest of the gay young matrons, smartly modern and worldly, told me with a touch of emotion of one of his talks on Keats.

"Stockton sees the world as it ought to be," she declared, "and you feel you're a hound-dog if you don't get out and slave to make what he sees come true."

What was it the old, old lady had said of Dr. Nathan Hoyt's sermons? "He showed us the fires of Hell, and then he swept our souls up to the gates of Heaven."

Stockton had omitted the hell fires, apparently, but for the rest, his grandfather's spirit was, quite evidently, still there.

"Stockton has many virtues, but he isn't domestically useful," Woodrow once remarked, and chuckled when he saw his family trying to hide their laughter.

For if ever there were a man domestically un-useful it was Woodrow himself. His one household chore was the Saturday night winding of the tall grandfather-clock, and I think he stuck to that task only because it gave him a chance to retell the old story of the Irishman in a clock shop. "This," said the salesman, "is an eight-day clock. It will run eight days without winding."

"It will, will it!" ejaculated the Irishman. "Faith, and how long will it run if ye wind it?"

On second thought, I am wrong! Woodrow on one occasion did a job which afterwards attained legendary proportions. It happened during their first year at Wesleyan when Ellen's Uncle Tom came for a week-end. Now Uncle Tom was a good bit of a swell, an Eminent Divine, pastor of a fashionable church in Philadelphia, married to a rich wife, living on a scale far beyond that of a young professor's one-Irish-maid-in-the-kitchen household. On the Sunday morning of that week-end, Woodrow, getting up early to fetch the newspaper, came upon Uncle Tom's boots outside the guest room door, large, handsome boots, custom made, muddied from a Saturday afternoon tramp in the woods.

Woodrow stared at them in dismay. The furnaceman, who might have been requisitioned, had come and gone, and Bridget in the kitchen would certainly walk out if she were asked to take on this duty. So Woodrow took the boots to the laundry, cleaned and polished them, and sneaked them back to Uncle Tom's door.

Years later, when he had just been elected to the presidency of Princeton, he and Ellen were discussing the enlarged staff which would be required to run "Prospect," the official house of the President.

I looked at him with a grin. "And who will clean the boots of the guests of the University?" I asked.

"The President of the University," Woodrow retorted.

As a matter of fact, during those early years in Princeton, Woodrow had no need to be useful, for Edward Axson was still there, and Edward could make anything and fix everything.

"Mr. Ed, would you be after taking a look at me coffee grinder?" Maggie would ask. "Mr. Ed, the sewing machine needs oiling," this from the seamstress by the day. "Will you mend my painting easel?" from Ellen. "My typewriter is jammed," from Woodrow. "My bicycle chain is loose," from me and the girls. Had the age been as completely mechanized as today, Edward would have had no time left in which to get educated. As it was, he managed to do all the odd jobs, neatly and deftly, his whistle, clear as a mocking bird's, rising above the noise of his tools.

"The boy is worth his weight in gold!" Woodrow declared fervently.

Occasionally old Dr. Wilson would look in on Edward in his improvised workshop, and watch the boy's activities almost with awe.

"To me it is one of the mysteries of the universe," the old Doctor observed one day, "to see two wheels fastened together and made to turn a third wheel."

One of Edward's gadgets delighted all of us. He was

a chemist and his laboratory work called for a lot of extremely accurate measuring of liquids, drop by drop. So Edward built a miniature Ferris wheel; each spoke of the wheel held a rack for a test-tube, and was supported by a nicely gauged trigger. When the required number of minims had dropped into the tube, the spring would be released, the wheel would revolve and the next spoke with its empty tube would slide into place.

"I'd like to keep the thing on my desk and play with it!" Woodrow exclaimed.

The truth of it was that Edward, with his scientific turn of mind, was a "sport," an accident, in this most unscientific of families. All of the other grown-ups were experts in their own lines: Woodrow in history and jurisprudence; Ellen and Stockton in philosophy and literature; Dr. Wilson, presumably, in theology. But science, pure or applied, left all four of them cold. Edward himself used to chuckle over his family's colossal ignorance, and no doubt a scientist from outside would have been immensely amused had he seen us standing in an awe-stricken circle while Edward performed his (to us) sleight-of-hand magic.

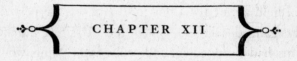

CHAPTER XII

THERE WAS one exception to the joint ownership of the in-laws which was so charming a characteristic of both Woodrow and Ellen. Old Dr. Wilson belonged to Woodrow and Woodrow belonged to Dr. Wilson. Th' ould Doctor, as Maggie the cook called him ("Th' ould Doctor do be wanting his eggs just *so!*") wouldn't have it otherwise.

"Uncle Joseph never loved anyone except Cousin Woodrow," a niece of the old Doctor's once remarked, and I suspect she was right. Certainly he wasn't lavish with his affections around the Library Place house.

When I first knew him, he was a good-looking, irascible old man with a Paderewski-like shock of white hair, and eyes like shiny black diamonds. My nieces stood in awe of their grandfather. And no wonder! One never knew where his next barbed shaft would fall.

"What is Joe doing now, Doctor?" Stockton asked one

day—meaning, of course, Joseph, junior, who had been a classmate of Stockton's at Wesleyan.

"He is editing a weekly newspaper down in Tennessee," the old Doctor replied, and added, with a sardonic twist of his lips, "He should spell it *weakly*."

After I had heard two or three such remarks, I decided that my best bet was to keep out of the old Doctor's path, and I succeeded fairly well until one unfortunate day when my vanity brought me into the field of his vision.

Ever since Meena's gift of scarlet shoes had broken me of the habit of walking pigeon-toed, pretty shoes had been my greatest weakness. It was a standing joke in the family, and one day Woodrow, passing through the hall with my brother Stockton, stopped in front of my open door.

"Come in here, Stock," he ordered, and crossing the room with exaggerated caution, he flung wide the door of my closet, and pointed to the neat rows of shoes—riding boots, sturdy brogues, flat-heeled pumps, and dancing slippers, gold and silver, green and scarlet.

"Good heavens!" Stockton exclaimed, his eyes bulging.

"Exactly!" Woodrow laughed, and then began to chant—

> "*A centipede was happy quite*
> *Until a frog in fun*
> *Said, 'Pray which foot goes after which—'* "

But the old Doctor didn't share Woodrow's tolerance of feminine vanity. I ran into him full tilt one evening when I was dressed for what in more sophisticated circles would have been called a sub-deb party. He looked me over from the red flower tucked into my braids to my high-heeled scarlet slippers.

"You women!" he exclaimed in disgust. "Why in thunder do you get yourselves up like popinjays!" (And I realized that only his ministerial cloth had kept him from using a much stronger word than *thunder*.)

I was flattered at being called a woman. But also I was furious. The mean, disagreeable old thing, I thought. I'd get even with him! I'd ignore his very existence and then perhaps he'd be sorry.

The old Doctor wasn't sorry. He seemed completely unaware of the fact that I was ignoring him, and it rather took the wind out of my sails. I was as friendly as a young puppy. Except for that one occasion when I had black-mailed Sally's beau into disgorging the money for the Minister's salary and he had scowled at me ferociously, I had never before run across anyone who apparently didn't like me, and the thing began to get on my nerves. Then I had a brilliant idea. I decided that he was a poor lonely old man, longing in his secret heart for kindness. All right, I'd be kind to him! All at once I became the charmingly attentive little granddaughter-in-law. I anticipated his every wish; I bobbed up with his box of pills and a glass of water; I tore upstairs to fetch his forgotten spectacles. One day I met him in the hall carrying a handful of letters. "I'll take them to the postoffice for you, Doctor," I said sweetly.

His thick eyebrows drew together. "You will not!" he

barked. "You'd forget them before you reached the corner—"

I glared at his retreating back, crowned by its saintly halo of white hair, and deep down inside me something told me that I might as well give up, that th' ould Doctor and I were not predestined to be intimates.

Perhaps the old Doctor was one of those strange creatures, a man's man who didn't like women around him. Although completely indifferent to his granddaughters and to me, he undoubtedly showed a surprising friendliness toward the two Axson brothers. He actually allowed Edward to mail his letters, and he and Stockton would sit by the hour on the porch or in the living room, talking, talking, talking. I used to wonder what on earth they found to talk about for such long stretches. Woodrow and Ellen would join them after lunch and in the evening, and my nieces and I would sit listening in demure silence.

I fancy that a student of heredity and environment would have found that group very interesting. Woodrow and Ellen and Stockton were all Children of the Manse, and although Dr. Wilson's father had been a newspaper editor and publisher, he too had been brought up in the Presbyterian way, had married a minister's daughter, and had promptly started a manse of his own. How had that Puritan heritage and their early environment shaped the characters and lives of those four so different people? I remember that Stockton often said of himself, "I may be a poor Christian, but I'm a mighty good Presbyterian!" Was it because he realized, in spite of the fact that his life had carried him far away from the manse, that he had never really escaped from the influences—nor even from the limitations—imposed on him by his church's discipline?

Dr. Wilson himself had been the most potent influence in Woodrow's young life. He had early recognized the unusual calibre of his son's mind and had done everything possible to stimulate and develop that mind. Looking over a boyish attempt at writing he would demand: "What are you trying to say?" And—"Then why in thunder don't you *say* it?" Also he had drilled the boy in the craft of public speaking. "Learn to think on your feet," he ordered. "Shoot your words straight at the target. Don't mumble and fumble." All of which must have been of incalculable value to a lad who was later to become one of the most distinguished writers and speakers in the country.

Dr. Wilson belonged to that group of ministers which the South always referred to as Eminent Presbyterian Divines. Both of Ellen's grandfathers had been Eminent Divines as had two of her uncles. Her father, although one of the ablest of them all, had died before he reached the age when a minister becomes "eminent."

I was never quite sure what constituted this divinity, but I very soon realized that the Eminent Divines rarely seemed to like one another. The Presbyterian hierarchy of those days must have been rather like a high-class club, the members of which knew each other or knew all about each other. Being human, they undoubtedly had the usual human prejudices and antipathies. Said Dr. Joseph Wilson of Dr. Thomas Hoyt, Ellen's uncle:

"Thomas Hoyt is the handsomest man I ever saw, but I never liked him. He's a wolf in sheep's clothing."

Said Dr. Thomas Hoyt of Dr. Joseph Wilson: "He's a born trouble-maker."

Occasionally serious differences of theological opinion developed in the hierarchy. The great Dr. James Woodrow, Woodrow's uncle, was one of the early followers of Darwin in this country, and a jury of his peers tried him for heresy. During the trial he was asked if it were true that he did not believe that Moses wrote the Pentateuch.

"Well," replied Dr. Woodrow in a tone of sweet reasonableness, "I find it difficult to believe that Moses wrote the portion which describes his own death."

Dr. Wilson, with his wit and his irascible temper and his Puckish sense of humor, must have been something of an *enfant terrible* in the hierarchy. It apparently never occurred to him to keep his opinion of his brother ministers to himself, and that tongue of his, that witty, barbed tongue, could shoot out missiles that hurt. Unfortunately, he didn't keep his barbs for the ministers. One day as he was driving down a street in the town where he was then living, an Elder of his church hailed him and stood leaning against the wheel of the buggy as they chatted.

"That's a fine horse you're driving, Doctor," remarked the Elder, and added jocosely, "It seems to me it looks better kept than the Minister."

"That is to be expected," retorted Dr. Wilson. "*I* take care of my horse while my congregation takes care of me."

No doubt remarks such as that had something to do with

his frequent change of churches. In addition, he had a restless strain in him, which would make him tire of a place and want to move on. He moved almost as often as a Methodist, while Ellen's two grandfathers remained for more than thirty years in their respective charges. It always amuses me when I hear Virginia claim Woodrow as a son of that Mother of Presidents. He was born there of course, but then he might just as well have been born in North Carolina or South Carolina or Georgia.

The truth of it is that Woodrow belonged to no state. He was, first and last, an American. But he was also a Scotch Covenanter. A writer, speaking of his fight for the League of Nations, points out that in choosing a word to describe it, President Wilson rejected "compact" or "alliance" or "federation," and picked "covenant" because he "knew well the moving effect that word would have in the minds of millions of Americans who had his own association with *Covenant* as a religious term."

To me it seems self-evident that he would have chosen "covenant." It was a familiar word to him and to my Aunt Louisa. Their forebears had belonged to that grim band who had fought and died for their right to freedom of faith. Neither Woodrow nor Aunt Louisa really *enjoyed* a fight for the fight's sake. They had none of the Irish zest in a free-for-all. But, like those old Covenanters, when their conscience demanded it they fought grimly and well.

Woodrow often told a story of another member of the ministerial clan. A tall, big-framed man, a "saintly" man, with a long silver-white beard that made him look like the pictures of God in mediaeval paintings. One day when he was buying a railroad ticket, the clerk became insolent. Instantly the old minister seized the man by the shoulders and dragged him, writhing and speechless with fright, half through the narrow ticket window. Then all at once the old Divine stopped, waited a second, then slowly, deliberately, shoved him back again and set him on his feet. "I beg your pardon, Sir," he said with a courteous bow. "I had forgotten for the moment that I am a Minister of the Gospel."

"And the Lord help that clerk," Woodrow would remark, "if he hadn't remembered just in the nick of time!"

These then were Woodrow Wilson's forebears. Men of learning and wit; fighters, who were ready to die for their faith; saintly men who occasionally "forgot that they were Ministers of the Gospel."

CHAPTER XIII

IN OCTOBER of my first year in Princeton, I went off to my new school, and my brother Edward to Massachusetts Tech, and we didn't see the family again until the Christmas holidays. My first Christmas in this new land.

The first thing about it that struck me as strange was that my nieces made no mention of the firecrackers they would shoot off on Christmas morning. How well I remembered Christmas in Illyria! I would get up before daylight, stand shuffling and impatient while my Aunt Louisa bundled me up in coats and heavy shawls. Then I would take a shovelful of hot embers from the banked fire, and rush out into the darkness. I would feel the cold creeping up under my little skirts as I knelt down and puffed and blew until the embers turned into a tiny bed of glowing coals. Then—bang, bang, bang!—off would go my first firecrackers. Sometimes I would recklessly set off a whole bunch at once, and the graying dawn would be streaked by tiny flames.

My nieces listened to me scornfully. Who ever heard of firecrackers at Christmas! If I hadn't been in bed with malaria last Fourth of July, I would know that that was the time for fireworks. I stared at them in amazement. At home in Illyria we had never paid any attention to Fourth of July. "We never bothered with Yankee holidays," I declared.

We hadn't known that Woodrow was listening to our argument, but when I spoke of the Fourth of July as a Yankee holiday, he suddenly came to life. His *George Washington* had been published a year or so before and no doubt he felt a sense of personal ownership in the Colonies.

"For heaven's sake, Ed," he said to my brother, "take her out and show her that American history did not begin with Sherman's march through Georgia."

So my brother took me out, and showed me the village from the point of view of history. He began with Nassau Hall, "Old North," to which the Continental Congress had fled after the British captured Philadelphia. In the main assembly room hung a picture of George Washington in a tarnished gold frame which once, Edward told me, had held a portrait of King George II. But during the Battle of Princeton a British cannon ball came through the stone wall of the building and neatly removed King George. Later some ardent patriot had installed the portrait of our own George, General Washington.

Out on the campus Edward showed me a cannon which had been captured from the British. He took me down a side street and pointed out a smallish stone building called the Old Barracks where a detachment of General Washington's soldiers had been quartered. Then we started out Mercer Street to the Battlefield. There I saw a second captured cannon, and on a near-by boulder an inscription which said that on this spot General Mercer fell. On the way back we passed a small cottage and stopped to read another inscription:

Thomas Olden House.

From the porch of this pre-Revolutionary house, General Washington reviewed his troops on their march to Trenton in December 1776. After the battle of Princeton he came here to seek aid for the British sick and wounded.

It had snowed the night before, in itself sufficient cause of excitement to the erstwhile resident of Illyria, but during our sight-seeing tour the weather had cleared. As we turned away from the Battlefield, I looked at the great cedars pricked out in white; at the wide, unmarred stretch of snow undulating off to the west where it seemed to meet and mingle and take color from the clear jade-green of the sky. I drew in a deep breath of the icy-cold air, and looked up at my brother.

"I thought I'd always be wanting to go back to Illyria," I confided, "but do you know, I think I sort of like Princeton."

Edward laughed and hit me with a handful of soft snow, and in a second we were rolling in the snow like two puppies.

The next day was Christmas. No doubt I received a

number of gifts, but I remember only two of them. A pair of real skates—ice skates, not roller—from my brother Edward, and from Woodrow a copy of his *George Washington*, inscribed to me in his own clear, beautiful handwriting.

Overnight, the child from Illyria, the Unreconstructed Southerner, had become an American.

Dr. Wilson had gone south before the cold weather set in, but Stockton was spending his holiday with the family, as was Helen; so the Christmas dinner was lively enough, although, like all the meals at the Wilsons, it was served with a touch of formality to which I hadn't yet grown accustomed. At my Aunt Louisa's, while everything was done nicely, it was done in the rather informal fashion of Illyria. If there were important guests present, Cindy could put on airs with the best of them. Otherwise, she felt perfectly free to express her opinion in any vital discussion that arose. And I doubt whether Aunt Louisa had ever tried to suppress her. They had shared many vicissitudes, those two, from the march of Sherman's soldiers to the long-drawn-out Battle of Margaret, and they were friends and co-workers, rather than mistress and maid-servant.

Certain of Woodrow's biographers have pictured his Princeton life as but one degree removed from poverty, seeking no doubt a contrast with his later prominence— Lincoln, the rail-splitter, moving from log cabin to the White House. That kind of thing.

As a matter of fact, the Wilsons always lived attractively. They were far from rich, of course. No professors were in those days (perhaps they aren't now), but even with the incubus of the in-laws, they had all of the comforts and a large share of the graces of life. Both Woodrow and Ellen were born of gentlefolk, and their home always showed it. Their attractive stone and stucco house was furnished with antiques from their two families. To cook the well-planned simple meals, they had Maggie trained by Mrs. Rorer through the medium of Ellen, and to serve those meals they had Annie, one of the most smoothly competent waitresses in Princeton. In choosing the guests for her dinners, Ellen often quoted the old maxim, "not more than the Muses, nor fewer than the Graces." In other words, around eight, the number which she considered ideal for general conversation.

Bliss Perry in his book *And Gladly Teach* has given a delightful glimpse of the Princeton of those days. It was a simple place, of course. A small old college set down in a beautiful small village. No clubs of any kind, except an embryonic Faculty Club; no automobiles to send people careering over the countryside; few diversions except what they found in their intercourse with each other. Small dinner parties were the chief form of entertainment, and the dinners were far from elaborate—soup, a meat course, salad, and a sweet, and sometimes even the salad was omitted. After dinner, instead of playing cards or going to the motion pictures—which as yet were unborn—they talked.

And how they talked! A few years ago Nell Wilson remarked, "When you think of the conversation we listened to as youngsters, don't you wonder that we can endure the gabble we hear today?" Princeton was famous for good talk. There were Woodrow himself and Bliss Perry, and President Patton, a wit of the first order. Winthrop Daniels with his wide sardonic mouth, and John Westcott drawling out some unexpected gibe. Later, after President Patton called him to the English department, Stockton Axson was added to the group, one of the most brilliant talkers of them all. When men such as these got together, it wasn't just a story-matching contest—although every last one of them was a masterly story teller—but they handled even serious things with a deft touch that gave no suggestion of heaviness.

I remember hearing Woodrow holding forth one day on the difference between northern and southern stories. He said that the Northerner wanted his story short, sharply defined, spurred quickly to the climax, while the Southerner preferred more atmosphere, more delineation of character, a more leisurely approach to the point, which would be all the more dramatic when thus developed.

In retrospect, it seems to me that Woodrow himself and Stockton Axson were shining examples of these two schools of the story-telling art. Woodrow, although not a Northerner, always made his stories swift moving, with a quick climax, while anyone who ever listened to Stockton's tale of a hunting trip in south Georgia, heard the southern method in its most perfect form.

Bliss Perry left Princeton soon after the time of which I am writing, and in 1902 President Patton moved over to the Theological Seminary, and Woodrow was elected President of the University in his stead. So that first group of famous "talkers" was broken up.

The other two, Westcott and Daniels, stayed on the faculty, until Woodrow as Governor of New Jersey appointed Daniels to the Public Utilities Commission, and later as President of the United States, transferred him to the Inter-State Commerce Commission. From the Commission Daniels went to Yale as professor of transportation. His was a distinguished career, fulfilling the promise of his early Princeton years. But the pressure of public affairs never robbed him of the sardonic turn of mind which had always delighted us. I well remember the last time I saw him. His wife was telling us of a bit of land they had bought in Connecticut where they expected to build when Winthrop retired. There was already one building on the plot, a small abandoned church which she planned to turn into a guest house.

"I think I can make it attractive," she said. "Fortunately it had been an Episcopal church, architecturally good and with a pleasing roof line."

Winthrop's wide flexible mouth twisted into its own inimitable grin. "If it had been a Presbyterian church, I'd feel more sure of the foundations," he observed dryly.

And I thought, with a backward glancing smile, "How Woodrow would have enjoyed that remark!"

Harry Fine was another member of the faculty who was a close friend of Woodrow's, one of that small group of college and classmates who always called Woodrow "Tommy." He was made Dean of the Faculty after Woodrow became President of the University, and throughout the eight years of that presidency, he was an unswerving supporter.

"Harry Fine is like Aaron upholding the arm of Moses," Ellen once remarked, and none knew better than she how to value such loyalty.

As the University grew, the duties of Dean became too heavy for one man; so the office was divided and a new Dean, the Dean of the College, was appointed. Said Harry Fine to the young incumbent of the new office, "I shall treat you as the President has always treated me, never interfering, and never volunteering advice, but always solidly back of you in any decisions you make." Which perhaps gives a clue to the successful administration of the University during Woodrow's presidency.

Dean Fine always took exception to the statement that Woodrow disliked anyone who opposed him. "We have argued and disagreed for years," he would say, "and we are still friends." Then he would tell of one occasion when, some question of policy having arisen, he had suggested calling a meeting of the Preceptors and sounding out their opinion. Whereupon Woodrow laughed and shook his head.

"It would be a waste of time," he said. "Every last one of them would agree with me except Blank, and he'd tell me I didn't know what I was talking about."

"And Blank," Dean Fine would point out, "was the one member of the younger faculty whom Tommy liked best and trusted most fully."

When Woodrow became President of the United States, he wanted to appoint Harry Fine Ambassador to Germany, but for financial reasons Mr. Fine refused and stayed on at Princeton as Dean of Science until he was killed by an automobile which ran into him as he was riding up Nassau Street on his bicycle.

Woodrow had always been the idol of the undergraduates, whereas Harry Fine as a young professor was their bane and terror. He was a brilliant mathematician and the undergraduate dumb-headedness drove him frantic—and he told them so in no uncertain terms. An old grad of the nineties once drew a pitiful picture of himself seated in the back row of Fine's Freshman Math.

"Back of me through the open door of the classroom, a cool breeze sent shivers down my spine; in front of me Harry Fine was mowing down the innocents, one by one, row by row. I sat there shivering and cowering, watching the swift approach of sudden death. Now he was one row ahead of me; now he had reached my row. There was no hope of last-minute salvation, for all of us back there were blockheads, not one of us could answer the simplest question. Two men in my row went down. I was the next—

"When I came to, I found myself in the middle of the campus, stuttering like an idiot. As Harry Fine called my name, I had swung myself over the back of the seat and vanished through the open door. I still don't know how I managed it!"

Next to Stockton Axson, John Grier Hibben, "Jack,"

was Woodrow's closest friend on the faculty. He, too, was a Princeton graduate, and had returned as instructor in logic in 1891, a year after Woodrow returned as professor of jurisprudence. I don't know when the friendship between the two began to develop, but certainly by the time I arrived at the Library Street house they were closely united.

Woodrow had never been a man of many intimates. I can count on the fingers of one hand the ones whom I happened to know. There was, of course, first and most important, his father, "the old Doctor"; Robert Bridges, his Princeton classmate, and Heath Dabney of the University of Virginia; Stockton Axson, his brother-in-law; and finally, Jack Hibben. I don't mean that Woodrow hadn't many *friends*. The six members of the class of 1879 who, together with Robert Bridges, always spent their class reunions in his house, bear witness to his power of friendship. But the five I have just mentioned belonged in the inner citadel of his heart.

In some ways, Hibben must have been even closer to Woodrow than was Stockton Axson. They were nearer of an age; they had been in college at the same time, and could exchange memories of those pleasant student days; they were both married men, and the joys and responsibilities of devoted husbands and fathers must have given them a sympathetic understanding which Stockton, the free-lance "old bachelor," could not share. Moreover, Jack's wife, Jennie Hibben, was almost as much Woodrow's friend as was Jack himself. Ellen and Jennie liked each other well enough, though they were never intimate. But then Ellen was even less given to intimates than was Woodrow.

Scarcely a day passed that Woodrow and Jack did not meet, even though only for a moment, and every Sunday afternoon the two Wilsons, the two Hibbens, and the two Bliss Perrys—as long as they remained in Princeton—had tea with Miss Henrietta Ricketts and her mother. In his *And Gladly Teach*, Mr. Perry recalls the talk on those occasions as having been "exceptionally good." They discussed literature and life in general, with Woodrow Wilson taking the lead.

Jack Hibben, while he was never one of Princeton's famous "talkers," must have been a pleasant addition to that circle. He was companionable and friendly, and the kindest man in the world. The undergraduates loved him. "Here's to Hibben, we call him Jack, The whitest man in all the Fac." So ran his verse in the Faculty song which the Seniors sang on the steps of Old North during the long spring evenings.

Stockton Axson joined the Princeton faculty in September, 1899, and during the following winter was suddenly stricken with acute appendicitis. There was no hospital in the village in those days and he was too ill to be driven over to Trenton. So a surgeon was hastily brought down from Philadelphia and the operation was performed in the Wilson house in Library Place.

Ellen, as it happened, was visiting her cousins in Savannah at the time; so it fell to Woodrow to keep my brother

Edward and me posted as to Stockton's progress. He wrote to both of us a number of times, long, detailed letters which would free our minds of anxiety. In one letter to me he told how Stockton, in the delirium of fever, delivered a "prose poem" on the subject of my Aunt Louisa's drinking well in Illyria. The dull *plunk* as the bucket hit the water far down in the darkness; the rope dripping with moisture, sliding through his hot fingers; the slow rising of the bucket to the curb, its metal bands turning to frosted silver when they met the warm air; then the icy water against his lips as he drank and drank and drank— Woodrow said that it made him thirsty just to hear him.

Stockton's delirium took another and unexpected form, —he wouldn't have Jack Hibben in his room. Jack, always kindness itself, came around every day to do what he could to help Woodrow, but as soon as he appeared in the doorway Stockton would call out, "I don't want you in here, you black traitor!"

Afterwards we teased Stockton about his violence, and he always looked sheepishly apologetic. "The strange quirks that fever gives a man's brain!" he would say.

We all thought it excruciatingly funny, that out of a world full of men whom he might have excoriated, Stockton should have hit upon Jack Hibben, the dear friend of Woodrow and of the whole family.

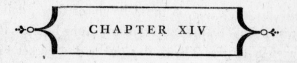

CHAPTER XIV

AT THE END of my first school year in the North, I returned to Princeton to find the family half buried in a litter of garments, and was told that we were going away for the summer.

Now the South of my day had not developed the habit of summer vacations, when everyone, from bootblack to banker, went off for two weeks or two months to recuperate from the arduous toil of the rest of the year.

Occasionally, it is true, someone would take a trip—to the Capital City; or to any exposition that happened to be in progress, or to New York or Washington, D. C. (We always spoke of it as Washington, *D. C.*, to distinguish it from the town of the same name in the next county.) Brides, if they were lucky, made their wedding journeys include both Niagara Falls and Washington, D. C.

Very rarely a fortunate individual went to Europe. And what a to-do there was when she returned! She invited all her friends to an evening party to see her collection of photographs and listen to her experiences abroad. Meena once remarked that her only reason for going to Europe was to keep other people from telling her about it.

But this notion of a whole family abandoning their home for the summer was new to me. I kept asking "Why?" and, "Don't you like it in Princeton?" But Ellen only laughed without bothering to reply, and my nieces murmured vaguely that "We most always go somewhere." Usually, it seemed, the Jersey coast had been their destination, but this time we were going farther afield, to Virginia.

Late one afternoon we drew up at a small country station far up in the foothills. A small boy stood on the platform and as we girls followed Woodrow and Ellen from the train I heard the boy counting—"One, two, three, four—good golly gosh!" he exclaimed and with the most disgusted expression I ever saw, he made off down the platform.

Later we learned what it meant. Woodrow, it seemed, had arranged for room and board for his wife and himself and four children, not mentioning our sex. And Sammy, the only child in the household and desperately lonely, had figured out that at least one of the four *must* be a boy. Poor Sammy, no wonder he was disgusted! I, too, accustomed to hordes of boy cousins in the South, was getting a bit fed up with so much concentrated femininity.

I was to have it still more concentrated here. The girls and I were given a large room in a wing and on two sides of the room were two huge four-poster beds. I, who heretofore had always had a room to myself, was now to share one with my three nieces. I decided that I didn't like this going away for the summer.

But that night I discovered under one of the four-posters a small "trundle bed," a kind of cot on wheels which was often used in the South to take care of extra children. With a whoop of delight, I rolled it out, mounted it, and steering with my foot against the floor, went tobogganing down the full length of the room, to bring up with a crash against the opposite wall.

On the next round I had a passenger, Nell; and on the third Marga-Jessie joined us. A long swoop, a crash, a shriek of joy from my passengers. Swoop, crash, shriek. Swoop, crash, shriek. Though I didn't know it, the old house was shuddering from the impact of those blows.

Suddenly the door opened and Ellen stood there frowning down at the four white-nightgowned figures huddled on the trundle bed. "Children! Have you gone crazy?" Then with a reproachful look at me, "I know who is responsible for this disturbance!"

I shrugged myself into bed completely spent. Was there never to be an end to this curtailing of my freedom!

Next morning Sammy eyed me almost with respect. "Golly!" he lamented. "Whyn't *I* think of that!"

Strange to say, I remembered Sammy's wail years later when Woodrow broke a hundred-year-old tradition by appearing before the two houses of Congress to deliver his address in person instead of sending it to be read.

Next day a cartoon showed a scowling Theodore Roosevelt, pounding the air with his fists and exclaiming, "Why in hell didn't *I* think of that first!"

Boys will be boys whatever their age or station.

It is interesting to recall that Washington and John Adams had both appeared in person, but Jefferson, being an awkward public speaker, had sent his address to the two houses.

The place began to grow on me. There was an easy-going atmosphere about it which reminded me of my own South. A wide board was missing from the floor of the back porch and all day long we unconcernedly stepped over the gap. One afternoon Woodrow was standing in the yard when I took the gap in a flying leap and drew up beside him.

He chuckled. "Someone once said that the keynote of southern character was the patient endurance of *avoidable* evils," he observed. "Five minutes and a handful of nails would replace that board, but no one has thought of doing it. And probably won't think of it all summer. I find it rather restful," he added.

He was right. When the September nip was in the air and we were ready to leave for home, we bridged the same gap on our way to the kitchen to say good-bye to the cook.

The house where we boarded wasn't one of the stately mansions of Virginia, but a big sprawling farmhouse set on a little knoll about three quarters of a mile from the station. A steep flight of steps led up to a narrow front stoop, and in a split-bottomed chair at one end of the stoop, the Colonel, our host, sat all day long whittling away at small cedar-wood slabs. He never constructed anything from those slabs. He just whittled.

Woodrow was a firm believer in whittling. "Whittlers are thinkers," he often declared. "Sitting with their chairs tilted back on the porch of a country store, or inside the store, gathered around the air-tight stove, they have time to meditate, to argue with one another. From such groups come the trickles of sentiment and conviction which merge at last to form the broad streams of public opinion."

So Woodrow now got himself a cedar slab and another split-bottomed chair, and joined the Colonel on the stoop.

The Colonel wasn't much concerned with the public opinion of today. He was still living in the period of the Civil War. Since Woodrow himself was something of an authority on that period, the two never lacked a subject for conversation. The Colonel knew every inch of the Virginia ground fought over by Marse Robert's soldiers. The opinions of experts he would brush aside peremptorily. "No, that is not correct," he would say. "Lee's men were *here*. Grant's *there*. I had been ordered to hold such and such a hill—" He was off, fighting again a long lost battle. One by one, the rest of us would slink away, but Woodrow sat on.

The Colonel had definite ideas on other things beside the War between the States. Ellen told one day of two women whom she had met in New York last winter, Miss Buckingham and Miss Gaines. "Miss Buckingham was from Virginia," she said.

The Colonel shook his head. "There are no Buckinghams in Virginia," he said flatly.

Ellen looked at him in surprise. "The foolish old man!" she thought. "Does he imagine he knows *everybody* in the state?" Aloud she insisted, "But she herself told me that she was a Virginian."

"Impossible," said the Colonel. "There is a Buckingham County, of course. But no Buckinghams."

A moment later Ellen had to back down. "I'm sorry," she said. "I've just remembered that it was Miss *Gaines* who was from Virginia."

The Colonel smiled benignly. "Oh yes, there are plenty of Gaineses. Blank County is full of them, and another branch of the family lives in the eastern part of the state. There are any number of Gaineses in Virginia, but no Buckinghams."

Woodrow's eyes twinkled as he looked at his wife's discomfited face. "Don't start an argument with an authority unless you are sure of your *facts!*" he advised.

While the Colonel sat on the stoop and whittled, his wife and her beautiful white-haired sister ran the house and the boarders. Did it well, too, giving the lie to their look of appealing helplessness. In these days of scarcity and rationing, I can scarcely bear to think of the food that appeared on the two long tables around which the family and the boarders gathered. For the midday dinner, there were always four meats—fried chicken, perhaps a leg of lamb, roast beef, and a Virginia ham which had been simmered in sherry and then baked. And the other meals were in proportion.

Evidently this family had not been burned out by Sherman, for the house was filled with beautiful old mahogany furniture. The patina on the dining room tables excited Ellen's admiration and the women of the household showed her how it was obtained. On a tree of the region, I think a locust, grew large bulbous lichens, with, beneath the hard outer skin, a spongy center fairly oozing natural oils. This oily sponge, plus "elbow grease," was the secret of the deep mellow glow of the mahogany. I have often wondered why these lichens weren't used commercially. Is it, perhaps, because the oils dry up when too long removed from the tree?

After a couple of weeks of high living, Woodrow announced that he was in need of exercise; so someone found a saddle horse which he could hire for five dollars a month with the saddle thrown in. We all gathered to watch him start off for his first ride. He was a well built man, with finely co-ordinated muscles, and in his linen clothes and leggings we thought he looked grand. Every inch a horseman, Ellen exclaimed.

The girls had never ridden, having been brought up in Princeton where saddle horses were not included in a professor's budget. But I had grown up with horses and I loved riding. When I pictured Woodrow cantering beside a little stream or ambling along shady country roads, I was almost sick with envy. But it occurred to no one, least of all to myself, to hire another horse for me. This was just one more thing that kept alive my homesickness for Uncle Warren and my Aunt Louisa and the place that in my heart I still called home.

However fate was about to intervene in my behalf.

On the third Sunday of our stay a seat was offered me in the church-going surrey, a privilege hitherto enjoyed only by the elders. I hadn't minded not going. Far from it! For after my years with my Aunt Louisa, I felt that if I never again entered a church, my average would still be high. But now I accepted politely just for something to do. The church was tucked away in the hills several miles distant from the Colonel's. We drove there through a pleasant countryside, did our duty by the service and returned. And that, I thought, was the end of the matter.

But that evening after supper, Ellen opened the door of our room and looked at me with a mischievous smile. "You are wanted downstairs," she said. "Brush your hair and come down."

Centering the house was a big hall which was used as a sitting room. The household was gathered there now, and when I appeared, Woodrow grinned and motioned me to the parlor on the left. I went on, and stopped short on the threshold. For inside the parlor, surging toward me, were five young men, ranging in age from seventeen to twenty.

I hadn't lived in the house with my cousin Sally for nothing. I knew what this meant. These were "callers," Sunday evening *callers* for *me!* I turned lobster red with shyness and excitement. "Oh, how do you do!" I stammered.

The tallest of the five stepped forward. "We saw you in church this morning, Miss Margaret," he said, "and we thought we'd drop around. I'm Kirby, and this is Lee. The fat slob over yonder is Tom, and the other two are Frank and Harrison."

By that time I had partially recovered. "But what are your other names?" I demanded.

They looked at each other and laughed. "Marshall," the tall one said, and added, "We're not brothers, Miss Margaret, but every second person in the county is named Marshall."

We were off to a good start. With our chairs drawn into a companionable circle, I forgot to listen to the voices of the elders in the hall. Those boys were darlings! They took control of the evening and of me, and gave me my first lesson in what every southern girl of that period had to learn—how to entertain a group of boys and make each one feel that she was interested in *him*.

They returned to the subject of their families. They were all descendants of the great Chief Justice and since almost everyone was named Marshall, they were usually designated by the names of their places. The father of one of these boys was Jim of the Everglades. Another was Jacqueline of the Crags. I was thrilled and showed it and that pleased them. Before the evening ended I was dated up for a "buggy ride," a picnic, and, joy of joys! one of them asked if I rode horseback and said that he would borrow his sister's mare and take me riding. I began to feel that this wasn't such a bad place after all.

At ten o'clock the Colonel's wife appeared in the door-way. The boys understood the signal, said good-night and departed. But I, when I had to face my elders in the hall, almost died of shyness. I ducked my head and scuttled past, but Woodrow reached out and stopped me. He too had once been a young Virginian paying a Sunday evening call on a girl. He looked at me with a smile of understanding. "Thus endeth the first lesson!" he said.

CHAPTER XV

AFTER MY school closed the next summer, I went back to Illyria for a visit. Uncle Warren met me at the station with his best horse hitched to a newly painted buggy, and before we went out to the house, he drove around the Square to show me off to his friends.

One after another they came out of their offices and stores to say howdy to Mis' Louisa's little girl. "Have you been a good girl, honey?" Colonel Saunders asked.

I nodded. "Of course! I'm always good now."

He chuckled. "When you start yelling up there in the North, I bet those Yankees think that Marse Robert's boys are coming."

"I don't yell any more," I said stiffly. "It's not nice."

That amused the two old men immensely. With his foot on the hub of a wheel, the Colonel began to reminisce. "Remember the Sunday Mis' Louisa let you take her to your church, Warren? Half way down to your pew you heard somebody snicker and looking back you saw her strutting down the aisle in her little red shoes with her red parasol wide open. You grabbed her, snapped down the parasol, and shoved her into the pew. Only time you ever made her do something she didn't want to do."

"Did I do that?" My newly acquired sense of what was fitting was horrified. "Oh Uncle Warren, I must have been *awful!*"

"I wouldn't say awful, exactly," Uncle Warren mused, "but it was always sort of interesting having you around."

It was a beautiful June day and the trees in the court house grounds were still freshly green. The clerk of the Court stood on the steps of the court house with his big dinner bell. "Oyez, Oyez, Oyez! The honorable the Circuit Court is now in session." The lawyers with their green baize bags were hurrying across the Square. It was all just as I had seen it hundreds of times, yet it looked strangely different. "Somehow the Square seems littler," I remarked.

"The Square's just the same, Baby," Uncle Warren said, a touch of sadness in his voice. "It's you who have grown bigger."

It was true. The tubby child of the Shorter Catechism days had shot up into a long-legged flapper. "She has longer legs and can run faster than any little girl I ever saw," Ellen's friend Miss Ricketts had declared during my last Easter vacation. I was fifteen years old now, and was to enter college in the autumn. I felt very grown-up with my mane of brown hair clubbed into a neat braid, fastened with a big bow at the back of my neck. I never thought of appearing on the Princeton streets without a hat.

But not here! I thought gladly. Not *here!*

Meena and the "Colonel" had gone from Illyria. He was a highly successful railroad lawyer now, and they lived in the Capital City. I missed them both terribly, but Aunt Louisa's big, cool, *empty* rooms welcomed me home. Here I regained the feeling of freedom that I had lost in the North. Aunt Louisa bought me some pretty ginghams at Illyria's best store, and my finicky northern clothes remained in the trunk. Sally's mare was still in the stable, a bit old now but still sure-footed and strong. I could ride to my heart's content. Only—Aunt Louisa decreed that I could no longer ride astride, as my brother Edward had taught me. Young ladies didn't ride cross-saddle in the South of that period, and I was now almost a young lady. So Uncle Warren outfitted me with an elegantly trailing riding skirt and a stiff hat. I was indeed grown-up.

Cindy didn't recognize that fact. "Yo' needn't be showin' off them uppity nawthern ways to me," she declared flatly. "I'se spanked yo' too often."

Neither did my Aunt Louisa recognize it except when she used it as a club to induce proper behavior. "Don't get notions, child," she would say. "You must put away childish things."

And I would retort blithely. "Anyhow you can't make me learn any new Bible verses, Aunt Louisa. I already know the whole Bible by heart."

Freddy, too, was home for his vacation from his priests'

school in Kentucky. We greeted each other across the hedge that separated the two places. "Hi, kid!" "Hello, Freddy!" We grinned cheerfully and went our separate ways. Gone forever was our offensive-defensive alliance. Freddy had his own gang now, and I, who had entertained real college students, couldn't bother with a gangling sixteen-year-old.

Friends in Illyria gave parties in my honor. "They're dancing parties," I warned Aunt Louisa, "and I dance all the time."

She sighed. "I suppose so. Ah well, you are out of my hands now. The responsibility belongs to Elly Lou." (I didn't dare tell her that Elly Lou was now called Ellen!)

Aunt Louisa and Uncle Warren could listen by the hour to my account of life in Princeton. "Dinner at night!" Aunt Louisa exclaimed. "Elly Lou must be crazy. It's a wonder you all don't die of dyspepsia."

She didn't like the sound of the German governess either. "I don't trust foreigners. Isn't Elly Lou afraid that she will teach those children heathen ways?"

I asked why she and Uncle Warren had never accepted my sister's invitations to visit her. Uncle Warren chuckled. "You couldn't budge Mis' Louisa, and I reckon I'd feel like a fish out of water up there with all those Yankees."

Though her approval of Ellen was tempered by different housekeeping methods, Aunt Louisa expressed only admiration for Woodrow. "It is a pity he didn't enter the ministry," she said. "Dr. James Woodrow's nephew couldn't be anything but a fine man. I was glad when Elly Lou married him, and I am still glad. It has been a good marriage. It is always well to marry a man you have known a long time, and whose forebears you know."

She had spoken like an oracle and I, just beginning to concern myself with human relationships, was impressed. When I got back to Princeton, I repeated her remark to Ellen. "Did you know Brother Woodrow a long time before you married him? I asked.

"Yes, and no," she replied laughing.

Then she told me how, a tiny baby, she had been taken by her mother to visit the Wilsons. Woodrow was at that time a small boy, with a normal boy's indifference to babies, but for some reason he had hung over Ellen as if fascinated. The family had laughed and called her his sweetheart.

Years passed. Dr. Wilson moved to another state, and the two children grew up without meeting. Then one spring Woodrow paid a visit to his cousins in the town where Ellen's father was minister. She was invited to supper to meet him and afterwards Woodrow escorted her home. (The colored servants undoubtedly said that he "carried Miss Elly Lou home"!) Returning, he stopped on the bridge across the river that separated the two parts of the town, looked down at the moonlit water, and told himself that he had met the one girl in the world whom he wanted to marry.

"He always says," Ellen concluded "that he had a unique experience. He adored his future wife as a baby and then fell in love with her at first sight."

It is not surprising that he fell in love with Ellen. My cousins in Illyria had told me that as a girl she was very slender, with big velvety brown eyes and hair that shone like a ripe chestnut. Since money was none too plentiful for a daughter of the Manse, she had evolved for herself an altogether charming costume to wear during the hot southern summer—a long straight frock of white muslin with a fichu knotted at her breast, white stockings and little black strapped shoes. She looked, said the cousins, as if she had stepped out of a Jane Austen novel.

"I stood all the girls in the world in a row," Woodrow told his small daughters, "and then I chose your mother."

Ellen, once started on their young romance, told me more of the young Woodrow. He had been a shy lad and when he went to call on a girl cousin who was a pupil in the seminary in the Virginia town where he lived, he would stand backed up against the wall, feeling himself awkward and ungainly; looking wistfully at those fluttering flower-like creatures, his cousin's school mates; longing to mingle with them freely as the other young men callers were mingling. He had a long, rather pale, lantern-jawed face, with grave gray eyes. Being a son of the Manse, he, of course, didn't dance, and he didn't know how to indulge in mild flirtations. The young ladies of the seminary turned aside from this solemn-faced youth and fluttered their long eyelashes in more promising directions. Even Woodrow's cousin felt slightly apologetic when she begged her friends to be kind to him.

At this point in her narrative, Ellen stopped and looked at me with a smile. "Did you ever hear of the girl who rejected an offer of marriage from the young George

Washington?" she asked. "Many years afterward she stood in her garden and watched him drive past on his way to be inaugurated as first President of the United States. It is said that she fainted dead away and had to be carried indoors and revived. I rather suspect," said Ellen, "that Woodrow's cousin has often come near to fainting!"

Ellen told me this story, remember, while Woodrow was still a youngish professor, bent on achieving a reputation in his own field, looking forward to no grand future in the public service. Yet even then Ellen quite evidently had no doubt that the sight of her married to Woodrow, was enough to make any woman envious. She wasn't one of the flirtatious nit-wits of the young ladies' seminary. She had a seeing eye. Woodrow often told her that the first thing to give him confidence in himself was the fact that *she* loved him. If she could look beneath his awkward exterior and love him, then, he felt, he must be quite a man!

Ellen's friend, Miss Henrietta Ricketts, once remarked, "If the doctor should tell Ellen that he could save Woodrow's life only by cutting off a piece of her flesh, she would look at him with her great brown eyes and beg, 'Be sure to take a *big* piece, Doctor!'"

Unfriendly biographers like to assert that Woodrow lived too much surrounded by women. That was far from the case during his Library Place period. The girls and I being still too young to count, Ellen really spent her life in the company of men. There were Woodrow himself and his father, and Stockton Axson (now a professor in the University with bachelor quarters on Nassau Street), who dropped in every day. Edward Axson and Woodrow's nephew, George Howe, were no longer in college, but they came back often for long visits, and there were still boy cousin students drifting in and out, and a preponderance of men guests. I remember most vividly Mark Twain and Walter Page and Robert Bridges, Woodrow's classmate and dear friend. Humphrey Ward, also, and another Englishman who looked embarrassed to death when confronted with four flappers, and who, I afterwards learned, was Lowes Dickinson, author of *Letters of a Chinese Official.*

They came and they went, all these men. Old friends and distinguished visitors, some of them drawn to Princeton by Woodrow's growing fame. My nieces and I were never present at the dinners given to these guests, but occasionally we were allowed to come into the living room afterwards, where, dressed in our simple little frocks we sat wide-eyed, listening to the fun and sparkle of Woodrow and his friends. We had our favorites among them, and some of them we heartily disliked, but they all brought richness and color into our young lives.

It goes without saying that our frocks were simple. That was one way in which Ellen taught us to economize. As we grew older we had one "good suit" a year, and one party dress, bought in New York or Philadelphia. For the rest, Katie, the seamstress-by-the-day, spent several weeks each spring and autumn "running up" our dancing frocks, of which we needed an almost unlimited number. And if I do say it who shouldn't, we looked rather nice in those crisp, billowing dance frocks.

In the South I had never been accustomed to showy clothes, and when I began to spend my own money, I soon learned to "cut my garment to fit the cloth." Marga-Jessie, accepted Ellen's restrictions without protest. But to Nell those Katie-fabricated frocks were a thorn in the flesh. As the youngest, she was always having to wear made-over things, and she insisted that her fate was beyond words horrible in that she inherited not only from one older sister, but from *two* who for a long time were dressed alike. Her account of the *two* dotted swiss dresses both of which were done over for her, and which simply wouldn't wear out, would have brought tears to the eyes of a basilisk.

Nell with her fine sense of the dramatic always liked to picture herself as the family's ugly duckling, ignoring the fact that no one with the bluest eyes in the world could ever have been "plain." Years afterwards a southern beau of hers asked a question which her father delighted to quote. "Miss Nell," queried the young romantic, "are your tears blue when you weep?"

Ellen loved Nell's blue eyes. She was proud of all her daughters. "Ellen's geese are all swans," old Dr. Wilson would remark, as she told some story of their doings.

Once, several years after this period, having just returned from a visit in the south, I remarked idly, "Cousin Hattie says that she's not bragging when she says that her daughter is the most beautiful girl in the world. She's only stating a fact."

Ellen bristled all over. "That's ridiculous!" she declared. "*Everybody* knows that Jessie is the most beautiful girl in the world."

Ellen was particularly pleased that Marga was developing her voice. That made three of this unmusical family who could sing. Marga, Edward Axson, and Woodrow himself, who had belonged to the glee club when an undergraduate in Princeton and who still sang to us occasionally. I have never been addicted to tenors, but I liked Woodrow's voice, light and untrained though it was, when he sang his favorite Scottish ballad:

> *So ho ye ho, ho ye ho, ho ye ho, ho,*
> *And who's for the ferry?*
> *The ferryman's strong, and the ferryman's young,*
> *With but a slight twist to the turn of his tongue,*
> *He's red as a pippin and brown as a berry,*
> *And 'tis but a penny to Twickenham town.*

My nieces and I listened entranced.

Just as the rest of the world counted for nothing with Ellen in face of her children, so the girls themselves would have been shoved into the background had she been compelled to choose between them and her husband. Woodrow was not the irritable type for whom the house had to be kept quiet lest "the master" be disturbed in his work, but had he been, she would have locked her daughters in a dark room without a shadow of compunction. I dimly sensed her utter devotion and I remembered my Aunt Louisa's remark, "a good marriage." In my growing interest in people, I began scrutinizing other married couples.

"Brother Woodrow," I asked one day, "why do you suppose Mr. Blank wanted to marry his wife?"

Woodrow clutched his head in feigned dismay. "Don't start that!" he ordered. "That way madness lies!"

He had a theory—or rather, he *said* he had a theory—that no man ever married a woman who wasn't beautiful or whom he didn't *think* beautiful.

"Some of them must have awful queer notions of beauty," I ventured, and Ellen, glancing up from her book, asked demurely: "How about Hartley Coleridge? *She is not fair to outward view, As many maidens be.*"

"Insufferable idiot!" Woodrow, who had not lost his southern idea of gallantry, dismissed Hartley Coleridge in disgust.

That was Ellen! She knew more poetry than anyone else in the world, and could always find a poem to fit any situation. Just as Aunt Louisa could always find a Bible verse, and as Woodrow and I could dig up a nonsense verse.

Later, many writers harped on his fondness for limericks, but as a matter of fact, his greatest love was for Gilbert and Sullivan. He had a cherished, well worn copy of *Bab Ballads*, and evening after evening he would read aloud to the delight of the girls and me.

> *Oh, I am a cook and a captain bold,*
> *And the mate of the Nancy brig,*
> *And a bo'sun tight, and a midshipmite,*
> *And the crew of the captain's gig—*
>
> *With a girl for him—and a girl for he—*
> *And one for you—and one for ye—*

And one for thou—and one for thee—
But never, oh never a girl for me!
Which is exasperating for
A highly susceptible Chancellor!

And, prime favorite of all, "The Duke of Plaza-
Toro"—

In enterprise of martial kind,
When there was any fighting,
He led his regiment from behind
(He found it less exciting.)
But when away his regiment ran,
His place was at the fore, O—

That celebrated
Cultivated
Underrated
Nobleman
The Duke of Plaza-toro!

This he would deliver with a melodramatic unction that
would have starred him in any production of *The Drunk-
ard*. He loved gay nonsense. He could play the fool
enchantingly. Had we thought of it, the girls and I might
have said of him as a friend of mine once said of her
husband, "He is like sunshine in the house."

But all this fooling was, of course, only the seasoning
to the solid meat. He was a tremendously hard worker.
There were his lectures at the University to be prepared
and delivered; endless faculty and committee meetings;
trips away from home for public lectures; and, above all,
there was his writing. I, busied with boarding school and
college, was never in Princeton during term time, but even

in vacation we youngsters really saw very little of him except at meal times and after dinner. Hour after hour we could hear the steady click, click of his typewriter from behind the closed door of his study. During this period he was writing his *History of the American People,* and since he had no secretary, he did most of the typing himself. I don't know why one of us girls didn't learn to type and do it for him.

Two years before, *Harper's Magazine* had paid him what was then considered a very high price for his *George Washington.* Woodrow used the money to finish paying for the Library Place house, the grounds of which Ellen took such pleasure in developing. It wasn't a large place, perhaps two hundred feet by one hundred and fifty, but Ellen was stuffing it full of young trees and shrubs. She wasn't a "dirt gardener" and she hadn't "green fingers" as had my Aunt Louisa and I, but she could get effect with plants as she did with her paints on canvas.

"I'm glad I'm not a millionaire with a big estate," she remarked one day dreamily. "It's such fun knowing all the plants in my garden."

"If you humped yourself enough, you could still know them," Woodrow pointed out.

The quiet home life in the Library Place house flowed on uneventfully, and I at least, who was away most of the time, did not realize that it was nearing its close. I knew, of course, that back in 1896, long before I came to live in Princeton, the University had celebrated its one hundred and fiftieth anniversary. Distinguished scholars from all over the world had been present, and the President of the United States, Grover Cleveland, had come up from Washington. A militia company had been formed among the students, uniformed in blue and orange like George Washington's troops, and my brother Edward, because of his training in military school, had been one of the officers. Privately, I wondered whether Grover Cleveland hadn't been struck by that young officer's appearance.

I knew, too, that Woodrow had been chosen to represent the faculty and that the subject of his address had been "Princeton in the Nation's Service," but in my mind that had counted for little when set against the marching of those orange and blue troops.

There were others, however, who thought differently. The University had been jogging along under President Patton's guidance (or rather his lack of guidance) comfortably enough for those who asked for nothing better. The standard of scholarship was low and sinking lower, but life was pleasant there, and after all what did scholarship matter?

But certain members of the Board of Trustees and of the faculty remembered their great president, Dr. James McCosh, and the visions he had had of Princeton's future. No longer just a small college in a pleasant village where a boy could spend four happy, carefree years, but a great University, a centre of sound scholarship, whose graduates would go out finely trained to take their place in the world, and serve their country.

On a certain fine June day in 1902 the trustees of the

University were meeting in Nassau Hall, and across from the campus old Dr. Wilson was sitting in his favorite barber-shop, swathed in sheets and towels. Suddenly the door burst open and the little tailor from down the street tumbled in. "Oh Dr. Wilson," he gasped, scarcely able to speak for excitement, "the trustees have elected Woodrow president!"

PART IV

❖○❖

The House of In-Laws
"Prospect"

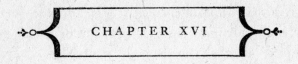

CHAPTER XVI

BACK IN the late seventeenth century three villages in a row had their small beginnings in the Crown Colony of New Jersey, King's Town, Queen's Town, Prince's Town. By some trick of chance, of the three, Prince's Town, or Princeton, became the most important, absorbing Queen's Town within its limits, and leaving King's Town an isolated hamlet on its outskirts. The post road between New York and Philadelphia as it passes through the village was called Nassau Street in honor of the Royal house of Nassau.

One Nathaniel Fitz Randolph owned most of the land on the south side of Nassau Street. To the north stretched the wide holdings of the Stocktons. Great builders, the Stocktons. The place is dotted with the houses they built for this son or that daughter, but the most important of those houses was Morven, seat of the Head of the Family, and still, to my mind, one of the most beautiful houses in

America. A certain Richard Stockton was the Head before and during the Revolution and was a Signer of the Declaration of Independence.

Across the road Nathaniel Fitz Randolph, so far as I know, built only one house, his own. But he gave a good-sized piece of ground to the College of New Jersey, and on the northern rim of that ground a large building of brown stone was erected and was called Nassau Hall or more familiarly Old North. In those days that building *was* the College.

Princeton, being thoroughly eighteenth-century English, drew a sharp distinction between the county families and the proprietors of the small shops that followed the line of Nassau Street opposite the campus. The tradespeople! At first the teachers in the College were likewise on the wrong side of the barrier. When a daughter of one of the County families so far forgot herself as to marry a professor, an old colored servant was not to be consoled. "Ain't it a shame!" she kept saying. "Miss Julia's done lef' de Quality an' married into de faculty!"

A vestige of that feeling still remained when the Wilsons first went to live in "Prospect." Ellen, interviewing a maid in a Philadelphia employment office, was told, "I've got a cousin cooking in Princeton," and when Ellen asked for whom the cousin worked, the woman replied, "Oh, it's nobody you'd be likely to know, Ma'am. Just one of them professors." Her face when Ellen told her that she, too, belonged to them professors, was a study.

Gradually the County families and the College merged

to form one social unit, but the division between Town and Gown still continued. None of the faculty "knew" the townspeople. None, that is, except Woodrow. Often as I walked with him down Nassau Street he would point to a handsome lad—"That's Blank's youngest son. Wouldn't he make a cracking good football player!" Or, "That lady is the druggist's wife."

It didn't seem strange to me. In Illyria—the tradition of the aristocratic South to the contrary—everybody knew everybody else, and one of my chosen intimates had been the daughter of our colored laundress. But one day it occurred to me that I never heard anyone but Woodrow so much as mention the townspeople. I spoke of it to him.

"Sheerest nonsense!" he exclaimed. "Snobbery such as that in America! Of course I know them—aren't they my fellow townsmen?"

That explains the little tailor's excitement over Woodrow's election to the presidency of the University. The Town looked upon him as *their* president. When, later, he attacked the system of undergraduate clubs, declaring that in their exclusiveness they were a menace to the democratic spirit which should prevail in an American university, the Town sided with him in the row that followed. But the County almost to a man and certainly to a woman, was against him.

The townspeople in their little stores and workshops were closer to reality than the old families. They knew the value of the thing for which Woodrow was fighting. And as one of them said, "By God, we're with him!"

Ellen, although she didn't know it when they moved into "Prospect," belonged to the County. Her grandmother, her father's mother, had been a Randolph, and since she had come from Virginia Ellen had taken it for granted that she belonged to the Virginia Randolphs. But with the approach of her middle years, when genealogical interest is most likely to develop, if ever, Ellen began delving into the history of her forebears, and to her astonishment she discovered that one of them had been that same Nathaniel Fitz Randolph who had made the first grant of land to the College and that his house had stood almost on the site occupied by "Prospect." The child of the grantor had come home.

"Prospect" itself had been built by the Potter family of Georgia as their summer home, but not, as might have been expected, in the white-columned southern style. It is more like a country villa in the Po Valley of Italy—a long, rather stately house of brown stone, with two-foot thick walls and a chunky square tower at one end. Inside, opening off the two-storey central hall, are big, high-ceilinged rooms which in the old days it must have been the devil's own job to keep heated.

One type of southern architecture the Potters retained. Each of the four large bedrooms had a small room next to it for the accommodation of a personal maid (the White House, too, features this same arrangement); and now Ellen was to be thankful for this feature, for without those small rooms, how in heaven's name could she find space for her family and the in-laws?

The house now known as the Dean's House, next door to the First Presbyterian Church on Nassau Street, had been built in 1756 to be the official residence of the President of the College. John Witherspoon, Signer of the Declaration of Independence, had lived there although he had also a place of his own, a beautiful old stone farmhouse called "Tusculum" a few miles outside of Princeton. Jonathan Edwards, the great Puritan, and father-in-law of the first Aaron Burr, was another distinguished President who occupied that first official residence. Other less famous Presidents followed one after another, and then in 1868 came Dr. James McCosh, in many ways the greatest of them all. He it was who transformed Princeton from a glorified boys' school into a real college, and undoubtedly his dreams and aspirations had a tremendous influence on Woodrow Wilson's career.

Under Dr. McCosh the College began to expand. New buildings appeared—Dickinson, the old school of Science, and Witherspoon. One can't say much for the architecture of the period, for without exception those buildings were hideous. Still, the mere fact that alumni and the families of trustees were moved to give them, showed that new blood was surging through the veins of the old College.

In 1879 the Potters sold "Prospect" to the College, and Dr. McCosh ("Jimmie" as he was affectionately called) was the first President to occupy the new official residence. The next four decades in the history of "Prospect" might be entitled the Saga of the Baths. During the McCosh regime, there had been one bathtub of painted tin enclosed in wood, set up in a room off the back hall. For the Pattons a second bath was added, this time in the small "maid's" room next to the southeast bedroom, and a third makeshift affair for the servants in a made-over pantry on the ground floor (although the servants' sleeping quarters were on the third floor!). Then came the Wilsons and yet another bathroom, while with their successors, I understand, baths sprouted all over the house like mushrooms. Thus do the luxuries of one generation become the bare necessities of the next.

The Wilson's Library Place house was almost a mile from the College and there, in complete seclusion, they had lived the simple life which was natural for a professor's family. Woodrow had bicycled or walked to his lecture room in Dickinson. Ellen, who was never any good as a walker, depended upon one of Guinn's "deep-sea-going hacks," as the students called them, when she had to pay calls or do errands in the village. Her three daughters walked or bicycled to their school.

For to the family's great delight Miss Fine, Harry Fine's sister, had opened a school for girls in Princeton, and having need of a language teacher, had removed the incubus of Fräulein from the Wilsons' weary shoulders. It was in every way a better arrangement. Miss Fine was a born teacher who would take her pupils up to college entrance examinations; the girls would be better taught than under the sole tutelage of Fräulein; moreover, surrounded by companions of their own age, they would lead more normal lives.

I, by this time, was nearing the end of my college course. I had entered at fifteen against Ellen's protests. "She's too young," she declared. "She should wait at least a year." But I was eager to go and Woodrow backed me up.

"She is well prepared," he pointed out, "and she will grow a year older just as fast in college as out of it."

So all four of us were now set for a real education. The Library Place house which we loved was gone forever. Henceforth our home would be a big house on the outer rim of a campus swarming with fifteen hundred students. "Prospect" was set in its own grounds, but those grounds were not enclosed. Undergraduates going from the dormitories to their upper-class clubs, took short cuts in front of or behind the President's house; on the days of big games with Yale or Harvard the whole population of the country seemed to stream past our doors. Woodrow lecturing to his class remarked that formerly he had likened the growth of tradition in government to a path across an open meadow, faintly discerned at first but year by year growing wider and deeper and more clearly perceived as the feet of the followers of the path passed over it.

"But I shall have to abandon that simile," he continued. "Last Saturday, just before the Yale game I saw eight distinct paths made across my wife's garden in the space of a half-hour."

It was that intrusion of the public on their privacy, a thing always precious to the Wilsons, as well as the presence of three young daughters and a young sister-in-law in the house, which made Woodrow decide to surround "Prospect" and its grounds with a tall iron fence. It was a handsome fence and it served well the purpose for which it was erected. No longer would we look up from our Sunday midday dinner and see faces of strangers pressed against the dining room windows. There were several gates in the fence of course, but they were cleverly placed so that the students would be taken well out of their way if they used them. The boys decided that it was simpler to follow the usual paved walks of the campus.

And what a tempest in a teapot that fence caused! Editorials appeared in the student papers. The freedom of the campus had been infringed upon, they said; the rights of the student body to walk where they pleased. The storm raged for days, then, suddenly, it was all over. The student body had exercised its right to grouse and grumble.

The matter of the fence, however, still lay in the future. During that summer of 1902 Ellen was busily doing over "Prospect," and heaven knows it needed doing! Her predecessors had been casual tenants and, in addition, the house still showed the results of its last orgy of redecoration under Mrs. Blank, the widow of an old-guard life trustee, who for some unknown and certainly unofficial reason, considered herself the custodian of "Prospect." The Pattons moved out and Mrs. Blank arranged to meet Ellen for a first tour of inspection.

Now Ellen was the sweetest looking thing in the world. Her eyes, beneath the thick brown hair, were soft and dark as brown pansies; the lovely rose color came and went in cheeks still softly rounded as a girl's; her voice had never lost its southern intonation. Bliss Perry, back from a firs visit to the South, had said of Richmond, Virginia, "Why, down there even the street-car conductors talk like Mrs. Wilson!" But Ellen's appearance was as deceptive as were my Aunt Louisa's mild blue eyes. For Ellen was not soft! Woodrow in a letter to me had once remarked that although Ellen was in bed with a heavy cold, her will power was still unimpaired.

She and Mrs. Blank stood in the big drawing room of "Prospect," a room of beautiful proportions, with high ceilings, and tall French windows. Said Mrs. Blank, "I think we shall take the rug for the key-note and build up the furnishings from that."

Ellen looked at the rug, handsome, no doubt, and costly, but her artist's eyes were offended by the garish colors. "No," said Ellen quietly, "I shan't use the rug at all!"

She looked at the horror of a mantelpiece, golden oak inset with a bevelled mirror which was flanked by a succession of small shelves supported by machine-turned spindles.

"The first thing I shall do," observed Ellen "is to tear out that mantelpiece."

Mrs. Blank stared at her in complete unbelief. "But Mrs. Wilson," she cried, "*I* chose that mantel myself the last time the house was done over."

"Did you?" said Ellen sweetly, "I never knew who chose it." (She was always so courteous and so firm!)

The battle was not won in a day. Mrs. Blank fought grimly for what she considered her rights, but at last she withdrew defeated. Meantime Ellen had brought down from Philadelphia a not-too-modern decorator, and together they had made their plans. With Mrs. Blank out of the way, the work started, and, as Ellen had promised herself, the first thing to come out was that spindled atrocity. An old inhabitant of the village recalled that formerly there had been a beautiful white marble mantel in the drawing room. It seemed reasonable that there should have been, since the mantels in all the other rooms were of marble, white or tawny gold or ebony black. But where was it now? The curator of grounds and buildings turned detective and started out on a still-hunt for the mantel.

Other old inhabitants confirmed the impression of the first. There had been such a mantel, unquestionably, but what had become of it no one could say. At length the curator came upon a clue. After the last redecoration of "Prospect," many of the things removed from it had been sold. The mantel, someone thought, had been bought by a rich old dowager in the village for five dollars. The dowager, approached, seemed to remember the purchase of the mantel, but hadn't the faintest idea what she had done with it. Certainly she hadn't installed it in her own house. Perhaps she had sent it to an orphans' home in which she was interested.

The dowager's colored butler had been listening to the conversation. "Scuse me, Ma'am," he said, "but I seed a crate of some sort down in our cellar. Maybe dat's what the genlman is wanting."

It was. There lay the lost mantel, still crated as it had

come from "Prospect." The dowager generously sold it back to the University for a hundred dollars, making a profit of only ninety-five. She probably felt herself cheated.

Many people thought that Ellen's drawing room in its soft tones of rose and beige was too formal. But Ellen felt that since it was intended for formal entertaining, it should *be* formal. Let the other rooms be homelike! Next to the drawing room was the smallish square room which was the ground floor of the tower. The ceiling here was so high as to be out of proportion, so Ellen had it lowered with a false ceiling. Next came the study, fortunately untouched by former redecorations. Ellen, too, left it as it was, almost as it had been in Dr. McCosh's time. Woodrow said that he had a vivid picture of himself seated beside the long flat desk opposite old "Jimmy." Woodrow particularly liked the bookcases in the study, tall, reaching two-thirds of the way up to the ceiling, shut in by pointed Gothic glass doors. They gave individuality and distinction to the room. These doors were removed by one of Woodrow's successors and now the bookcases stand blatantly open. They look well enough of course. To my mind, phalanxes of books always look well. But the room has lost its distinction, and it is no longer the study of "Jimmy" McCosh and of Woodrow Wilson. It seems a pity!

Across the large square hall were the dining room and the library, which the family used as a sitting room. Here Ellen had put the furniture from her Library Place living room, and here we would linger for a bit after dinner, talking over the happenings of the day. Or perhaps Woodrow or Ellen would read to us for an hour. Then we would separate for our diversified amusements of the evening.

The family settled into its new quarters. Woodrow and Ellen had the big southwest bedroom with its connecting "maid's" room. Jessie and Nell shared the room over the library; Marga's was on the narrow hall that led from the stair landing to the billiard room. I, when at home, would be in the room that was the second floor of the tower. It was farthest removed from a bath and had no closet, but to compensate for its inconveniences Ellen turned over to me the third floor of the tower, opening off the attic, where I could store my surplus belongings and feel that I had a place of my own. The top of the tower extending above the roof with a window on each of its four sides, Woodrow later took for his own private retreat. When he was up there he was "out," not to be interrupted for anything less than a life or death emergency. It was in that tower room that he did all his important writing of this period, and I in my own room below him could hear the sound of his typewriter going on and on.

Another old inhabitant of the village told us of the marriage of one of the Potter daughters. When she stood at the foot of the really grand staircase, the train of her wedding gown reached all the way up to the landing. That fired the imagination of the girls and me, and we began to plan our own weddings. We couldn't hope to rival the Potter girl, of course, but perhaps we could run to trains *half* as long as the staircase. Little did any of us dream of the so-much-grander house in which my nieces' weddings were destined to take place.

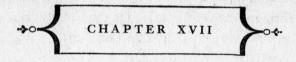

CHAPTER XVII

I WENT BACK to my college soon after the Wilsons moved into "Prospect," but when I returned for the Christmas holidays I realized that the atmosphere of the University had changed. I met a young professor hurtling across the campus as though the devil himself were chasing him. "The good old easy-going Patton regime is gone forever!" he grinned as he drew up beside me.

The students, too, felt the difference. When an unheard-of number flunked the midyear examinations, a cartoon appeared in the Princeton *Tiger* showing Nassau Hall festooned with cobwebs and Woodrow in cap and gown alone on the front steps. Nobody left in the College but the President! The caption beneath the cartoon read WIL-SON, THAT'S ALL, taken from the slogan of a well-known brand of whiskey.

The mortality had been especially high in an art course which up to now had been the cinch of all cinches. An athlete who simply had to have a few additional credits always took it, knowing that whether he attended the lectures or not, he would pass. Now of a sudden he hadn't passed, and that spring a new verse appeared in the Faculty Song which the Seniors sang on the steps of Old North—

> *Here's to Frothy, our latest find.*
> *He's gentle and easy to drive and kind.*
> *But he had to make his courses hard*
> *Or he couldn't play in Woodrow's yard.*

And still another verse queried—

> *Here's to Blank, our Prof retired.*
> *Did he quit or was he fired?*

That Faculty Song, by the way, had made its first appearance soon after Woodrow joined the faculty. Several of the older professors had been outraged, declaring that it must be stopped at once. But Woodrow, a graduate of the University of Virginia law school and at one time a practicing lawyer, told them that it couldn't be stopped. As a result, the Seniors sang blithely—

> *Here's to Woodrow Wilson, O*
> *Our legal adviser don't you know.*
> *He says they can't stop us, so let 'er go.*
> *Here's to Woodrow Wilson, O.*

That tightening of the standard was the first of many changes. President Eliot had long ago established the free elective system at Harvard, and other universities had followed suit. A student could elect any course that he chose, with the result that his four years of academic life were often a hodge-podge of unrelated subjects. (It must have been rather like the progressive schools of today!)

But now Princeton under its new president was about-facing. After a Freshman year made up almost entirely of required courses, a student could choose his subject—classics or government or English literature, or some branch of science. Then, the *subject* once chosen, his *courses* were fairly definitely planned. So many in his own particular field; so many in related subjects; so many unrelated, in order to give breadth to his education.

Years later when my husband and I were living in Berkeley, California, the public press announced that Harvard was abolishing its free elective system, having come to the conclusion that it resulted in an unbalanced education. The faculty of the University of California was at that time largely composed of Yale graduates, with one lone Harvard man in the English department. The Yale men at once began to rag him—"So Harvard at last has decided to educate its students!" they jeered.

He bore it in silence for a time, and then came back at his colleagues. "Yes, Harvard at last has decided to educate its students. And Yale will watch the experiment with intense curiosity!"

My husband and I, hearing of Harvard's decision and the ragging, smiled in our sleeves. Woodrow had beaten Harvard to it by almost twenty years!

After he had abolished the free electives, Woodrow started in with something never before attempted in an American university, the preceptorial system. In the autumn of 1905 fifty new men were added to the Princeton faculty. *Preceptors,* who were to meet the students informally in small groups of five to ten, work with them, still informally, discuss and argue and stimulate their minds. It was a grand scheme, and, strange to say, it worked. The men chosen were the pick of their fields all over the country and it is interesting to note how many of that first batch of fifty have attained distinction in their own lines.

And what a thrill the advent of the Preceptors gave to the girls of Princeton! Fifty new men at one whack. *Fifty!* Some of them showed up with wives, of course, but most of them could be classed as dancing bachelors, and we saw to it that they danced. There weren't many girls in the Princeton of those days. A few belonging to the "old families"—Stocktons and Scotts and Hodges; a few daughters of professors; and my three nieces and I, who had gone or were still going to school and college but were home for vacations. We were all, of course, still of an age to enjoy the students, their big Proms and the small dances in their club houses. Nevertheless, we didn't turn up our noses at the Preceptors.

With the appearance of a horde of young men, some of whom might conceivably turn into serious suitors, Woodrow showed a hitherto unsuspected side of himself. He turned into the conventional father who dislikes his daughter's beaux. He might have thought well of one of his young Preceptors, his training and ability, but if the young man began to haunt "Prospect," Woodrow at once lost his taste for him. And—to a lesser degree, of course—he felt the same distaste for my beaux.

He was too clever to say outright that he didn't like the chaps. There were other subtler ways. By degrees all the steady callers at "Prospect" were given special names. One of them was known as "Chronic," he being like a chronic disease in the house. Another became "Mr. Brook," for while men may come and men may go, the brook "comes on forever." Another was "Old Faithful"—"he spouts every hour on the hour."

"It's a miracle that any of us ever got married!" Nell said laughingly years later.

As a matter of fact, I was the only one of us who married a Preceptor, and that not until long after he had stopped being a Preceptor.

One day as I was passing through the hall Woodrow called to me from his study. "Nell is seeing a great deal of young Blank. Do you think she is seriously interested?" he asked with a touch of genuine anxiety.

I laughed. "Not in the least! She's only feeling her oats."

Woodrow looked relieved, as though the Voice of Authority had spoken. "I am glad. I can imagine no worse fate for a girl than to marry a man of coarser spiritual fibre than herself."

The swiftly passing years had brought changes to the House of In-laws. Old Dr. Wilson died, to the deep and lasting grief of his son. Edward Axson and his former roommate George Howe were both married and out in the world. The number of boy cousins who were students in the University had dwindled to one.

"Is Le Foy popular with his classmates?" Ellen asked, interested in this cousin.

"I judge so," Woodrow replied. "He sits in an end seat in my lecture room, and every chap who passes hits him on the head with a book."

There still remained Stockton Axson, still the bachelor professor living in his own rooms on Nassau Street and turning up at "Prospect" every day. We were all thankful that Stockton was already a member of the faculty before Woodrow became president. For if there were one thing which Woodrow detested more than another, it was any form of nepotism.

His nephew, George Howe, had taken his degree in classics at Halle in Germany, and returned to America shortly after Woodrow had been elected president. The Latin department wanted George as an instructor but Woodrow said, "No! Not my nephew."

After he became President of the United States, this attitude was even more marked. There was the young man who had come back from Germany to be Woodrow's assistant. He had taken his degree in international law, government, theory of the state. He had worked with Woodrow for almost ten years, and since Bryan, who had to be Secretary of State, was woefully untrained in those subjects, Woodrow needed as Solicitor of the State Department someone whose abilities he knew and could trust.

"It is too bad," he said to a member of his Cabinet, "that

the one man in the country whom I should like to have as Solicitor is the one man I can't appoint because he is my brother-in-law."

He was often condemned for this attitude. To appoint a relative to an important post just because he is a relative, is obviously bad, his critics contended. But to refuse to appoint a well trained man just because he is a relative is equally bad—almost worse, since it deprives the country of much needed services. Myself, I am inclined to agree with Woodrow. After all, no one man is indispensable, and it is better to lean too far backward than to fall forward on one's nose. Nell, of course, evaded this difficulty. Mr. McAdoo was already Secretary of the Treasury when she married him, and Woodrow couldn't very well dismiss a member of the Cabinet simply because he had married his daughter.

The men guests who came to "Prospect" were different from those of the Library Place house. There they had been relatives or friends or scholars attracted by Woodrow's personal reputation. In "Prospect" they were more apt to be guests of the University. Every Saturday a clergyman arrived to preach in the University chapel on Sunday. They came from all over the country, from every religious denomination, and taken by and large were as interesting a lot of men as one would care to meet. There were other distinguished visitors. James Bryce (not yet Lord Bryce) came for a lecture, as did Josiah Royce, President Lowell of Harvard, Sir Gilbert and Lady Mary Murray, and swami-like, white-bearded Hiram Corson of Cornell who apparently went off (or into) mystic trances from which only Ellen or Woodrow himself could rouse him. Of Ithaca Corson remarked, "It is nine months Siberia and three months hell." And of his college, "The men students are unappreciative hyenas."

After Mr. Corson left there arrived a large packing case filled with a complete collection of his works, each book inscribed to Ellen in Latin: "Small, but a token of a not small friendship." Since she had never laid eyes on him until that week-end, Ellen looked somewhat startled, Woodrow chuckled, and the girls and I went off into fits of laughter.

Sir Gilbert and Lady Mary Murray arrived one evening shortly before dinner. Several members of the faculty had been invited to meet them and Ellen had planned a particularly nice menu. The first course was clear soup. Lady Mary refused it. Second course, sweetbreads. "No thank you," said Sir Gilbert. Third course, broiled squabs. "Thank you, no," said Lady Mary.

At that Woodrow turned to her in dismay. "But Lady Mary, you are eating nothing!"

She looked at him with her peculiarly attractive smile. "Didn't you get my letter?" she asked.

"I got your letter, certainly, but I remember nothing that would explain your not eating," said her bewildered host.

Lady Mary laughed. "It is simply that we are vegetarians—"

Needless to say, for them the fourth course was *eggs*,

hastily prepared and brought in by a somewhat flustered Annie.

At the end of the evening, when the local guests had departed and the Murrays were safe in their own rooms, I saw Woodrow heading for the study and I trailed after him, suspecting what was in the wind. There it was, a note in Lady Mary's firm, "English" handwriting, neatly filling the first page of a small sheet of note paper. But at the bottom of the page, after her signature, appeared three letters in small capitals, *P.T.O.*, which Woodrow hadn't noticed before. Now he turned over, and read on the second page—"In case you should plan to honour us with a fatted calf, I had best tell you that we are vegetarians."

Woodrow and I looked at each other and burst out laughing. "By the great horn spoon!" he said.

The great horn spoon reminds me of Andrew Carnegie, who stayed at "Prospect" before and after he presented the University with a lake. That gift almost broke Woodrow's heart. With all the things the College needed—new buildings, endowment for professors' salaries, new scientific equipment—to be given a *lake!* The donor, red-faced and complacently beaming, turned to the president expecting full-voiced gratitude.

"Mr. Carnegie," said Woodrow gravely, "We need bread and you have given us cake."

Between Carnegie's first and second visits to Princeton, Woodrow had stayed at his place in Scotland, Castle Skibo, and on that occasion each guest had been presented with a horn spoon with which to eat his porridge. Very grand spoons, new and shining, with the name of the castle in silver. Back at "Prospect" Woodrow continued to use that spoon. Every morning he would take it up with a flourish— "Here's to the Laird of Skibo and his confounded lake!" he would say with a rueful grin.

But someone must have pinched pennies on those spoons. Little by little, the horn lost its lovely patina; then it began to peel off in flakes. At last, when it had attained the bilious color of a segment of dry mustard, it went into the discard.

So far as I know, Carnegie was the only "Prospect" guest who had been invited in the hope of luring from him a donation for the University, and that invitation had been engineered by one of the trustees. Dr. McCosh had been an adept at extracting money, at times from none too enthusiastic donors. Once, speaking to a group of alumni, he declared that he had never asked for donations. When the shout of laughter from the alumni had died down, the old Doctor, with a twinkle in his eye, continued, "No. I just present the needs of me College."

Andrew West, Dean of the Graduate School, was also expert in presenting the needs of his college. *Here's to Andy three million West*, sang the Seniors. *Sixty-two inches round the vest. At getting money he is the best—*

Woodrow was no earthly good at it. He insisted that the obligation of raising funds belonged properly to the trustees, while the president should be left free to run the college. Moreover, in addition to his convictions as regards the duties of a college president, he was temperamentally unfitted for the task of raising money. Normally a man of easy gracious manners, when confronted by a possible donor, he became shy, ill at ease, as embarrassed as though he were about to ask for money for himself. It takes a fairly thick skin to be a good beggar, however worthy the cause, and Woodrow was anything but thick-skinned.

CHAPTER XVIII

IT IS DIFFICULT to say when the girl Margaret began to develop a critical sense. Children seem to take their elders completely for granted, and Woodrow had belonged to the Axson family almost as long as I had. To me he was as much a matter of course as the house I lived in, or the suns of summer and the rains of winter.

But with the removal to "Prospect," the balance of power between men and women seemed to shift, and Woodrow now lived surrounded by women. To begin with, my nieces and I being almost "grown-up," there were five women in his immediate family, his wife, his three daughters, and I. His sister, Mrs. Howe, and her daughter, little Annie, paid visits of longer duration. Ellen's friends, Lucy and Mary Smith, from New Orleans, whom we met during that summer in Virginia, were almost a recognized part of the family. The girls called them "cousin," and they came to "Prospect" every autumn for a stay of several weeks. Of the boy cousins, students in the University, who once had blown in and out of the house like a fresh breeze, only one remained.

In the old days, Woodrow had been a fairly frequent visitor at the faculty club, the Nassau, which, before it transferred to its present attractive house on Mercer Street, had its quarters in the old ramshackle University Hall. Woodrow liked to play billiards, and two or three times a week he would stop by for a game and stay for a chat with one or more of his friends. The legend of his inaccessibility had not yet developed. He was never the back-slapping, jovial type, but he mingled easily with other men. As an undergraduate he had sung on the glee club. He had belonged to a group known as the "Witherspoon Gang" from the name of the dormitory where they lived. As a law student at the University of Virginia he had been asked to join one of the two swagger societies composed of the young "bloods" of the University; and certain it is that had he been a dour, self-centered "grind" he would not have received a bid to the "Eli Bananas" or the "Tilka."

But now the picture had changed. Most college presidents at that time did not bother with teaching, but Woodrow, in order not to lose touch with the students, continued to meet his Junior-Senior class twice a week at eleven o'clock in the morning. But because of the President's office hours his afternoon classes had to be abandoned and that meant no more stopping by the Nassau Club after his last lecture. Also, at about this time the club moved to its new house, and instead of the comfortable, rather shabby old place of three rooms, it became a modern club with a large increase in the number of members, many of them being alumni; food and drinks were served; a "ladies' day" was instituted, and the whole atmosphere was different. If Woodrow did drop in occasionally some man was sure to buttonhole him with a "If you will give me a few minutes now, Dr. Wilson, it will keep me from bothering you to-morrow." Woodrow, having gone to the club for relaxation, was forced to talk business, with the result that he very soon stopped going. And one more easy contact with his fellows was cut off.

The office hours were held at first in "Prospect," and beside the front door in a small wooden frame was a printed notice which said that the President, unless otherwise prevented, planned to be in his office between such and such hours on such and such days of the week. My husband tells me that certain of the faculty objected to that notice. They wanted to feel free to drop in on the President at any hour that suited them. Then when Woodrow's class gave '79 Hall to the University and he transferred his office to the big room in the tower, the same professors objected to that. The old easy informality was gone, the place was being run like a cut-and-dried business, they said.

The trouble was they couldn't get it through their heads that a big university *is* a business, and that the man at the head of it, if he is to be successful, must conserve his time and energy. For Woodrow this was especially true. Never of robust physique, he had learned not to fritter away his strength.

All of this, I think, goes far to explain the popular belief in his inaccessibility which must have had its origin at about this time. The whole business was unavoidable, of course, if he were to keep on doing his job, but it was unfortunate in that it forced him to seek his relaxation more and more with his few intimates, and with his family. And his family, as I have said, was now almost exclusively women. I think, too, that this increasingly feminine atmosphere must have prevented a beneficial hardening of his already too thin skin. I don't mean that we "pampered" him. He wouldn't have stood that for a minute, but as the only man in a household of women (three of them adoring daughters) he missed the toughening that tough-hided sons would have given him. He no longer had even Edward Axson's realistic, down-to-facts, scientific viewpoint.

Probably my own critical sense was born during this period. Naturally I had no pre-vision of what future critics were to say, but as I saw the two rows of smiling women at the dinner table and Woodrow, the lone man, at the head, it somehow seemed to me not quite normal, and I often said to myself, "There are entirely too many women around this place!"

Ellen, too, felt it, I think. One Christmas she gave him a billiard table and installed it in a big room in the east wing, hoping that he would invite his friends or that they would drop in for a game uninvited. But it didn't turn out as she planned, and before very long, Katie Murray, the seamstress by the day, was cutting out our dance frocks on the billiard table.

"I am submerged in petticoats!" Woodrow himself often declared laughingly, but that did not mean that he felt himself a fish out of water.

The average American man finds it difficult to believe that another man can like a woman for any but one reason. To Woodrow Wilson friendship between a man and a woman was as much a matter of course as between two men. He liked clever women. He liked their gaiety and wit; their power of skimming lightly across the surface of things. His women friends were, of course, as different as his men friends, but they had certain things in common. They were women of brain and heart and understanding. "She had besides beauty a most lively and stimulating wit; such a mind as we most desire to see in a woman. A mind that stirs without irritating you; that rouses you yet does not belabor; amuses yet subtly instructs." Thus Woodrow himself, as a young man, had written, and that was what he found and valued in the women who became his friends.

First in point of time among them was Elizabeth Bennett of *Pride and Prejudice*. He read very little fiction but what he did read, he took seriously. I remember the summer when one after another we buried ourselves in May Sinclair's *The Divine Fire* until in due course it reached Woodrow. One evening the maid came into the study with a card bearing the name Joseph (something) Keith, and Woodrow, looking up from his book, thought for a second that the caller was Savage Keith Rickman himself, the poet of *The Divine Fire*. With such power of externalizing a character in fiction it is not surprising that Elizabeth Bennett should be to him quite as real as any of the flesh and blood friends whose wit and enchanting gift of laughter so delighted him.

One of the first of these real life women was Mrs. Toy of Cambridge. Another was Mrs. Hibben of Princeton. A third was Mrs. Harry Reid of Baltimore who a few years ago published a delightful volume of her memories of Woodrow. Still another was an English woman whose name I forget, whom Woodrow and Stockton Axson met during a bicycle trip in England.

And then, of course, there was Mrs. Peck!

Mrs. Peck came into the public limelight several years later, but into our lives during the "Prospect" period. Woodrow, recovering from a heavy cold, was ordered into a warm climate to recuperate and he decided to go to Bermuda. He begged Ellen to go with him, but it was always hard to budge Ellen. "I must stay with the house, like the fixtures," she would say. So Woodrow went off to Bermuda alone. Near his hotel were the houses of several winter residents of the island, English and American, among them the house of Mrs. Peck.

Now Woodrow was always good company, a fact which the general public seems to find difficulty in believing. Just last winter the wife of the Princeton jeweller told me of seeing him get off the train at Princeton Junction late one afternoon. He was then Governor of New Jersey and she was surprised to see him unattended, still more surprised when no car met him.

"I took my courage in both hands," she said, "and asked if he wouldn't let me drive him to the village. And," she added, in pleased reminiscence, "we had the *best* time!"

Just so that winter colony in Bermuda must have had a good time when Woodrow joined them, and between him and Mrs. Peck sprang up that friendship which later was to have such repercussions. He spoke of her often when he returned, and read aloud to us her delightful letters. In one I remember, she spoke of the intense blue of the Bermuda sea reflected on a gull's wings. Woodrow looked up. "She is a keen observer," he said, "but I wonder whether that is possible."

In the early spring she came down to "Prospect" for a few days before going to her summer home in the Berkshires, and I liked her from the first. She fitted herself into the family group. She was gay and entertaining and interested in our doings, a woman of the world, not beautiful, but giving the effect of beauty. The women of Princeton at that time were not smart-looking, and Mrs. Peck was nothing if not smart. She wasn't accustomed to faculty circles and the difference between their clothes and hers made her vaguely uncomfortable. Dressing for a tea one afternoon, she called me into her room. "Do you think this frock is too extreme?" she asked with a touch of anxiety that I thought very appealing.

"Goodness, no!" I assured her. "You look lovely."

Later in the summer, Ellen and Woodrow and Jessie

went to her for a week-end. I was asked but unfortunately I was already dated. On their return Jessie remarked casually that they hadn't met Mr. Peck, but we attached no particular significance to his absence. He was, we understood, a successful New England manufacturer, absorbed in his business, with no time for winters in Bermuda and summers in the Berkshires. Somehow we got the impression that he was much older than his wife, a grim man, with grown daughters. If I gave any thought at all to the unseen Mr. Peck, it was simply in line with my old query about apparently mismated couples: "Why do you suppose Mr. So-and-So wanted to marry his wife?"

The next spring Ellen and Jessie went to Italy with Lucy and Mary Smith of New Orleans and I was in nominal charge of "Prospect"—Maggie and Annie, of course, really ran it. One day an out-of-town man with whom Woodrow had an appointment telephoned that he couldn't make it. That left Woodrow with a free afternoon on his hands. "Let's go have tea with Mrs. Peck," he suggested at luncheon. "She is staying with her friend Mrs. Roebling in Trenton."

There were few automobiles in the Princeton of those days, and we of course didn't own one. We took the old Johnson trolley at the foot of Witherspoon Street, and went jouncing across the pleasant countryside, chatting companionably. It was unseasonably warm and we had tea on the back porch of the big old Roebling house. Woodrow was a hard-working man, with heavy responsibilities. It was now almost the end of the college year and he was tired.

The gay talk of Mrs. Peck and her friend refreshed him. They took his mind off his work, made him laugh. On the trolley going home he remarked thoughtfully, "It isn't *only* the Marthas of the world who help!"

During the next year or two, Mrs. Peck came to Princeton fairly often. She became the norm by which we measured smartness. I, in a fit of extravagance, bought a more than usually swagger hat, and Ellen glanced at it approvingly.

"It looks like Mrs. Peck," she remarked.

Occasionally Mrs. Peck and the Wilsons met in New York for dinner and the theatre. Occasionally she and Woodrow alone, or with a friend, or with her son by her first marriage. During our last summer in Old Lyme, Woodrow returned from a few days in New York, spent chiefly with George Harvey and his political line-up. But he had found time to take in the circus in Madison Square Garden with Mrs. Peck and her friend. They all three doted on slap-stick comedy, and there had been a famous clown whose antics delighted them. Woodrow laughed heartily as he told us about it. Then he handed me a small tissue-wrapped package.

"This is a wedding present from Mrs. Peck," he said. "She says that you are to have it mounted any way you like."

The package contained a huge square-cut topaz, brilliant as a yellow diamond. I knew at once what I would do with it. I had bought during my last stay in Florence a topaz and silver-gilt collar, the center stone of which had

never pleased me. It was too small, too lustreless. I sub-
stituted Mrs. Peck's golden gleaming jewel, and there it
still remains.

I married, and a couple of years afterward my husband
and I moved to California. In the summer of 1915 Stockton Axson was lecturing at the University of California.
Seated on our brick terrace overlooking the great Bay, he
told us of the whispering campaign that was sweeping
across the country. Mrs. Peck and her husband, long out
of sympathy with each other, had decided on a divorce, and
Woodrow's political enemies had seized on that as a starting point for their calumnies. An injured husband, betrayal,
revelation, divorce. The whispers said that Mrs. Galt, who
was to marry Woodrow in the autumn, had bought off Mrs.
Peck with a large sum of money.

Stockton's voice grew more and more grim as he told
us. My husband and I grew more and more angry. Then
suddenly, all three of us shouted with laughter. It was
infuriating, but it was also completely and utterly *absurd*.

"They are making him out the most *efficient* man in the
world," Stockton observed drily. "Here he is, the head of
this great country which is teetering on the edge of war,
and yet in the midst of his great burdens, he has time for
this foolishness!"

The whispers never reached the public print. Theodore
Roosevelt not long before had brought suit (and won it)
against a newspaper which had accused him of intoxication.
Warned by that, no doubt, the whisperers against Woodrow
stayed underground. But the whispers grew and grew. The

shocking thing to me was the realization of the number of people who *wanted* to believe the scandal. Men and women whom we would have thought friendly to us listened to and repeated the stories with avid, gloating eyes. But with this unpleasant revelation of human nature, there came others surprisingly pleasant. Andrew West, Dean of the Graduate College at Princeton and Woodrow's bitter opponent in the "quad" fight, heard the gossip.

"Heaven knows I hated Wilson like poison," he said flatly, "but there's not one word of truth in this nonsense. It is simply not in character."

The whispers gradually died away, or at least we no longer heard them, and Mrs. Peck vanished from the public eye, the victim of conscienceless politics. I have always thought that the best refutation of the gossip would have been to publish in full the letters which she and Woodrow wrote to each other during the years of their friendship. They were both masters of that almost lost art. Their letters were gay, witty, thoughtful, reminiscent, revealing the sympathy between them. In addition to the scotching of ugly rumors, such a volume would have been a contribution to literature.

Many people were surprised that Woodrow did not marry Mrs. Peck after he was left alone by Ellen's death. They had been such friends, so congenial. And it seems to me that it might have happened had he met her for the *first* time after Ellen had died and before he met Mrs. Galt. As it was, the relationship between them was already crystallized in the definite form of friendship. During

Ellen's lifetime there had been no "Vacant" sign on Wood-row's heart. Afterwards, it took someone not associated with the old days, someone entirely new and different, to draw him away from his great grief into a new, different, yet very happy marriage.

CHAPTER XIX

ALL HER LIFE Ellen had longed to see Italy. She had been abroad more than once with Woodrow, but always in the summer, his only free time, when the Italian climate was too hot. Now she consented to leave Woodrow and her household gods, take Jessie, and join Lucy and Mary Smith in their projected trip.

Once the decision was made, Ellen plunged into an orgy of preparation. Not of clothes and such—heavens no!— but of reading up on Italian history and art. Evening after evening she sat with her pretty face buried in a book. She had the greatest power of concentration that I have ever seen. When she was absorbed in a subject, the house could have collapsed and she wouldn't have noticed. I often tried to attract her attention. "Sister," I would say. Then louder and louder, "Sister! *Sister!*" Or one of her daughters might call "Mother!" No response.

But let Woodrow speak to her in however low a tone,

and she would look up instantly—"Yes, dear? Did you want me?" As though, deep down inside her, there were a tuning fork that vibrated only to his voice. She would always hear him, I thought—her *heart would hear him and beat, had she lain for a century dead.*

Ellen had planned to return in good time for Commencement, but in Assisi Jessie fell ill with diphtheria, and they were held there until well into June. And now my game of housekeeping assumed a formidable guise.

In addition to the usual Commencement activities, I had to arrange for the garden party for the Seniors, the Trustee luncheon, and to entertain in "Prospect" Woodrow's seven classmates who, since his return to Princeton, had spent every reunion in his house. I wanted to remain in the background, directing the caterers from a distance, but Woodrow insisted that I appear at these functions as his hostess. Moreover I had the extra-curricular activities suitable to my age. I would dance all night, eat bacon and eggs with a crowd of boys and girls in a student's room, and then turn up at "Prospect" to give Woodrow and his friends their coffee.

"Aren't they wonderful!" I said to myself often. "To be so witty and entertaining when they are so old and so near the grave!"

When the seven, later on, sent me a wedding present of a gorgeous Kirke silver water pitcher, inscribed "To the young hostess of our twenty-fifth reunion," I was startled to realize that at the time they had seemed to me so close to desuetude and death, every last one of them had been several years short of fifty!

Jessie recovered from the diphtheria with no ill effects. They returned, and I handed over the keys of my temporary office with a sigh of relief. But all the talk of Italy had made me restless. When a certain Miss Thorp, who had lived most of her life in Florence, offered to chaperone me, I accepted joyfully. (Chaperones were still extant in those days!) I planned to stay a year at least, perhaps longer, and friends and relatives outfitted me as though I were about to become the first settler in a desert. There were knitted garments of every kind, which I carefully hid in Ellen's attic. There were bedroom slippers and hot water bottles, even a soft wool blanket which was supposed to cover the Italian hotel beds and protect me from germs —or worse. Ellen gave me a carefully selected case of medicines—the idea being that there were no drugs in Italy. And Woodrow turned up with a tiny silver flask which held about a teaspoonful of brandy. Also he handed over to me his old brown and tan steamer rug because it matched my "going away suit," and he himself had a new one straight from Scotland, in the plaid of his clan, the Campbells of Argyll.

So off I went to Italy for the first time. I never forgot my first sight of Genoa and the statue of Columbus. In those hands had lain the beginning of my country. *In fourteen hundred and ninety-two, Columbus sailed the ocean blue*, the Susie Carter Seminary for young ladies had taught us. And here was his statue facing the great stretch of water across which he had sailed to discover America. And here, as a result of that sailing, was I, and back yonder in America were my Aunt Louisa and Woodrow.

It was strange how often I thought of those two. Listening to High Mass in St. Peter's, I kept seeing the tiny little church in Illyria, and my Aunt Louisa sitting in her hard wooden pew with her bland blue eyes fixed on the young Minister. I remembered her wrath when the Minister had "spoken to" Freddy and me from the pulpit, and I laughed. Our misbehavior would have gone unnoticed here. Children were tumbling all over the pavement of St. Peter's, gnawing hunks of bread and garlic, enjoying little games of their own while their elders knelt devoutly in prayer.

As the great organ boomed out, I all at once remembered Woodrow's description of a service in old St. Giles in Edinburgh. He had stood outside the church door watching a regiment march down from the Castle, kilts swinging, bagpipes skirling. "What regiment is that?" he asked a man near him.

The man looked at him in deepest scorn. "Dinna ye ken the *Black Watch?*" he demanded.

Then Woodrow had gone inside and had heard the Black Watch singing, with no organ accompaniment, *God of our fathers, be the God Of their succeeding race.* And he had felt, he said, the racial tie between himself and those men. The God of their fathers, was the God of Woodrow's fathers. And, as I realized suddenly, of my Aunt Louisa's fathers. And, strangely enough, of *mine.* Never was I so close to becoming a Calvinist as during that first year in Italy.

The next spring I went north with two English friends, up the Adriatic coast to Venice, where I was to leave them and join other friends in Switzerland. On my last after- noon in Venice, I dropped into St. Mark's for a good- bye look, and there, sitting in a dimly lighted side chapel, to my surprise I found myself sobbing. I couldn't under- stand it. I had been a grand yeller in my youth, but never a weeper. Perhaps I was tired, I thought. We had travelled fast up the coast; our sight-seeing had been ferociously intense. Perhaps, too, I was sad at leaving Italy. Whatever the reason, I continued to sob, kneeling with my face hid- den in the curve of my arm.

I felt someone beside me and looked up to see a lean old monk in the brown robe of a Franciscan. "Daughter," he said in Italian, "you weep. You are in trouble?"

I mopped my eyes with a handkerchief that was already a wet ball. "I think not, Padre," I replied, and added, irrelevantly, "I am Protestant, Padre. I am Calvinist."

His old face creased into a smile. "What matters it, daughter?" he said. "Protestant or of the true faith, this church is the house of our Lord."

I left next morning for Switzerland, and a fortnight later as I sat in the garden of our hotel the *piccolo* came out with a fistful of letters, and stood with round, expectant blue eyes. Waiting. I knew what he wanted. I tore off the American stamps, gave them to him, and watched him bounce off down the path, his absurd little duck's tail coat sticking out over his fat rump. One by one I read my home letters. The last was from Ellen. She plunged in without preamble—"It is useless to try to break it to you gently,—" On that day when I had knelt sobbing in the chapel of St. Mark's, my brother Edward and his wife and baby son had been drowned.

Before me, a carpet of blue forget-me-nots swept down to the blue lake; beyond the lake towered the snow mountains. I stared at them with blank eyes. But I must have seen more than I thought, for in none of the gardens that I have since tended has there been a sprig of forget-me-not.

It was hardest of all when I reached "Prospect." Ellen wanted to talk, and I couldn't talk. She wept and I couldn't weep with her. She showed me a box of things that had come from my brother's home in the South. Among them was the dress I had made for the expected baby. I wasn't fond of sewing, but my Aunt Louisa had taught me well. It was a nice little dress, of fine handerchief linen with tiny hemstitched tucks in the yoke. I took it and gave it to the laundress whose daughter had just had a baby girl.

"How could you!" Ellen sobbed. "How *could* you!"

One afternoon as I came up the front walk, Woodrow saw me and called me into his study. It was then that he told me of the older sister whom he had loved.

"It is one of the most perfect of human relationships, when it is perfect," he said. "Your brother is gone, but you have had a beautiful thing."

He began to speak of the small boy Edward who had come to them soon after he and Ellen were married. Of the sweetness and strength that had lain behind the small-boy pranks. Of the pleasure he had found in watching the development of Edward's fine and finely disciplined mind.

"He had all the virtues I could have wished for in a son of my own," Woodrow said. "Even the virtue of not being too good."

He was sitting behind his big desk, I in a big chair facing the tree-dotted front lawn. I noticed vaguely that the grass had turned golden in the light of the setting sun. Something was happening inside me. All these weeks since Ellen's letter had reached me in Switzerland, I had been tortured by the thought of my brother fighting for the lives of his wife and little son, for his own life. Fighting and failing. Drowning.

Now, as Woodrow's quiet voice went on and on, the horror was leaving me. Now I could see again the brother I had known, slim and vividly dark in his gold-buttoned school uniform. The brother who had taught me to ride, with whom I had climbed trees and waded brooks. The college student with whom I had wandered over the Princeton countryside. I had him again, my brother.

I looked up and met Woodrow's clear gray eyes. "Thank you!" I said.

All my life he had been to me another brother; for the greater part of my life an almost-father, but of all the gifts of understanding that he had given me, that hour in his study was the greatest.

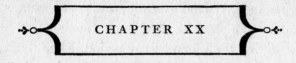

CHAPTER XX

IN THE OLD days in Princeton, a few wealthy families with big houses on the outskirts of the village owned elegant-looking victorias drawn by spanking teams of horses, bay or brown or bright chestnut. The rest of us rode our bicycles or walked or hired one of the one-horse surreys which the students called deep-sea-going hacks, and Mr. Guinn was the owner of the largest fleet of these hacks.

He was a remarkable man, that Mr. Guinn. Of British birth, with manners that could have given points to Lord Chesterfield, he was interested in American politics and was a political leader among his peers. He was also a diplomat of the first rank, the originator of the "Share-the-Ride" slogan. He had a limited number of hacks and an almost unlimited number of calls. He knew the exact route his hacks would take to reach their destinations and the houses they would pass on the way. It resulted in strange combinations. Two dowagers who had barely spoken to each other for a month would find themselves cosily ensconced side by side on the back seat of Mr. Guinn's hack. Two girls, in bitter feud over the same young man, would be decanted at a party like two bosom chums.

Once during the Library Place period, Ellen received a hastily written note from Mrs. Bliss Perry (telephones were almost non-existent in those days) begging her to "fill in" at a dinner party. Miss Juliana Conover had been invited, but not having heard from her Mrs. Perry assumed that she must be out of town. Now an unbalanced dinner table was anathema in those days, and Ellen, sensing her friend's need, rose to the occasion and sent one of the girls on her bicycle to order Mr. Guinn.

He came at the appointed time, assisted Ellen into the hack and seated her beside—of all persons!—Miss Juliana Conover. So off they went together, the unheard-from guest, and her substitute, and Mrs. Perry's dinner table was more "unbalanced" than before.

When there was sufficient snow to warrant the exchange, Mr. Guinn's hacks gave way to sleighs, and then our fun began. Leaving an afternoon party, the Winans girls, one of the Stocktons, and I would stage a chariot race down a snowy hill. We never dared try it with Mr. Guinn himself, but his five young sons were more amenable. The rawboned old horses would catch the excitement and, with ratty tails arched, would go racketing along amidst shrieks from the young contestants. Occasionally a narrow-bodied sleigh would tip over and slide us, all party-clothed as we were, into a snow drift, but the snow was soft and since none of us used make-up in those days there was no danger of smearing our faces.

We fondly imagined that our racing proclivities were unknown to our respective families, but one day an unguarded remark from me brought a twinkle to Woodrow's eyes. "Yes," he said, "I happened to be walking down Mercer Street late this afternoon." He gave me a conspiratorial grin and said nothing more, then or later.

It was not for nothing that Woodrow's father, the old Doctor, had owned a better horse than any of his congregation. Woodrow, too, knew a good horse when he saw one. And it was not accident that brought him and me together on the sidewalk curb to watch the start of the annual sleigh race down Nassau Street to the Prep School. This was a Town, not a Gown race, since the faculty couldn't afford horses, and the leading tradesmen took part in it. It was a fine sight. The neat little cutters, the trim horses, the men in their bright-colored sweaters. Then the starting signal, and they would be off with a swish, the snow foaming back from their runners. Woodrow would linger for a bit after the sleighs had vanished, chatting with the people around him. He knew all the men who were racing, knew who had won last year and who was likely to win this. I liked his looks as he stood there, so keenly alert, so friendly, his gray overcoat and gray scarf deepening the gray of his eyes. One among his fellow townsmen. No doubt his interest in their sporting event, added to the Town's feeling that he was *their* President.

Much has been written about Woodrow's health and even more misinformation has been passed along by word of mouth. Just the other day a woman told me that a bootmaker told her that President Wilson had a deformed foot which barred him from any kind of exercise. The bootmaker knew it for a fact for he himself had made the shoes which the President wore. What stories get about! If any bootmakers did work for Woodrow, it was in half-soling his perfectly normal, run-of-the-mill shoes, not in producing custom-made footwear.

As for the exercising part of that story, Woodrow always took more exercise than did the average professor. He was never an athlete, of course, but he was an excellent horseman and a conscientious though never an enthusiastic golfer. At certain periods of his life, he was an ardent bicyclist. More than once he and Stockton Axson bicycled throughout the length and breadth of England and Scotland. And I well remember the hours that Edward Axson spent trying to teach Ellen to ride so that she might accompany her husband and brother on their next bicycling trip. Woodrow would stand on the sidelines during those lessons, cheering her on, urging her to persevere, at their close picturing the fun they would have when they could go wheeling off together.

Later, when automobiles had made the roads uncomfortably crowded, Woodrow gave up bicycling, but he never lost his love of walking. His usual brisk constitutional at the end of the day was around Princeton's "little triangle," about two and a half miles, after which he would perhaps drop in on Miss Ricketts or the Hibbens for tea. Perhaps Ellen would meet him there and they would stroll home together in the late twilight.

He had a finely co-ordinated but not a robust body, and he had learned to discipline that body as he disciplined his brain. Ellen gave especial care to his food; he himself to his hours of work and relaxation. Above all, he had the gift of sleep. When we were on summer vacation, the girls and I declared that Woodrow, alone, did not hate a rainy spell because he slept as long as it rained.

That gift of sleep and that smooth co-ordination of nerves and muscles and brain probably helped him escape the "nervous breakdowns" which are so much featured in academic circles. Many professors seem to think themselves lucky if they manage to hold out until the Easter vacation; if they last through Commencement, it's a miracle. Stockton Axson, in spite of his good brain and good sense, was especially given to these breakdowns. I remember on one occasion, after he had again succumbed and been declared *hors de combat,* Ellen spoke of it, a touch of impatience mingled with her sympathy for her brother, "Can you ever imagine Woodrow giving way to such foolishness!"

He had illnesses, of course. The usual winter colds, rather fewer of those than the rest of the household in appallingly overheated "Prospect." He had a slight operation for phlebitis—and afterwards spoke of himself as "flea-bitten." Once, after an illness which they feared might be serious, all five of them went to England for a long, restful summer in the Lake country, where Ellen almost froze and the rest of the family flourished. Woodrow always seemed to take illness in his stride with no nervous after effects.

Back in the nineties, according to my husband, it was said that after lecturing to his class, Woodrow would be compelled to go home and lie down for an hour. I know nothing about that, but certain it is that in the Library Place house as I knew it, and later in "Prospect," there was never an atmosphere of illness or semi-invalidism. Woodrow and Ellen, to the outward view at least, were always serene.

After I finished college I became definitely a part of "Prospect," leaving it only for trips abroad and visits in the South. The in-laws still came and went, of course, but I find my memories centering more and more on Woodrow and Ellen and my nieces. We lived a pleasant, friendly, well-ordered life, with no trace of the quarrels and upsets which are so marked a feature of some families. I, accustomed to my Aunt Louisa's rule that, unless you were sick enough to be "physicked," you must appear at the breakfast table properly clothed, was usually the first down in the morning, with Woodrow a close second. He would come into the dining room not too annoyingly cheerful, drink his fruit juice, and while the thin slices of bread were browning on the electric toaster, he would glance over the morning paper, making running comments on the headlines. Then with a look of mock dismay, he would shove his egg in its silver cup over to me, for to his abnormally sensitive finger tips the heat of a boiled egg was torture. I would laugh and with a clip of a knife neatly remove the top, add pepper and salt and return it, now sufficiently cool for him to handle with ease.

By that time Ellen and the girls would have drifted in one by one and we would settle down to the usual family discussion of plans and engagements for the day. What I wish to emphasize is that there was never any friction at that breakfast table. Woodrow, with a full schedule before him, could always be sure of a pleasant beginning to his day. And that must have meant a lot to a sensitively organized, hard-worked man.

After the meeting at breakfast, my next most vivid memory of Woodrow is on the "Prospect" terrace in the late spring afternoons. When I came in from a canoe trip or a horseback ride or a walk with my current beau, Annie the maid would bring the tea table (and I mean *tea!*) to the western end of the terrace onto which opened the French window of the small tower room. Pretty soon I would become conscious of movement behind me and over my shoulder would glimpse Woodrow making a careful reconnaissance to see who this particular young man might be. If it were someone he didn't care for, he would disappear without more ado. Otherwise he would join the party and make himself so delightful that I am sure my beau bragged about that hour for days.

After the young man had departed, the real treat began for me. Woodrow would lean back on the wicker divan, reach for his second cup of tea, and begin to talk. I said very little during those sessions, but I listened, and odds and ends of his talk come back to me.

Someone proposed to open a kindergarten in Princeton for the faculty children. Woodrow didn't like kindergartens. He didn't believe in *luring* children into the paths of education. He wouldn't drive them, of course, but he would make them understand the difference between work and play. He would say, "Now children, put away your playthings and get to work."

A few years ago I quoted that remark to a friend who was once the head of a successful school for small girls— *not* a kindergarten.

"He's dead right!" she exclaimed. "There is entirely too much softening up of character in this country. Besides," she continued, "children like to feel important, and when you tell them to stop playing and get to work, they almost burst with a sense of importance."

Woodrow declared that to know that you could do a thing well was not conceit. To illustrate this he told a story of his friend, Dr. Maltbie Babcock, at one time pastor of the Brown Memorial Church in Baltimore, afterwards of the Brick Church in New York. During the weeks he was lecturing at Johns Hopkins, it was Woodrow's habit to attend the morning service at Brown Memorial and afterwards join Dr. and Mrs. Babcock for midday dinner at their house. One Sunday, however, he arrived for dinner without having first attended church. Dr. Babcock listened to his expressions of regret and then exclaimed,

"It's too bad you weren't there. You missed a cracking good sermon!"

"That wasn't conceit," Woodrow said. "It was simply a

statement of fact from a superlatively fine preacher who knew that he had preached a superlatively fine sermon."

Woodrow once declared that if he had belonged to the body of churchmen who decided which were the seven deadly sins, he would have placed selfishness very near the top of the list. If you weren't thinking first of yourself you wouldn't commit murder for money, or for revenge. You wouldn't steal another man's wife, or abscond with his fortune. You wouldn't plot against the state unless you thought you yourself would derive profit from your treason.

An English woman whom I had known in Italy was one of Mrs. Pankhurst's first suffragettes, and for a year or so seemed to spend at least a third of her time in prison. During the whole of this period she sent me the official organ of the suffragettes, *Votes for Women.* One afternoon while Woodrow and I still lingered on the terrace, Annie brought out the mail, and mixed in with the letters was a newly arrived copy of that rather badly printed little paper. Woodrow took it up and glanced through it. He wasn't opposed to votes for women *per se,* he said, but he felt that in many cases it would only result in the doubling of the vote in each household—a useless enlargement of an already over-large electorate.

During his first or second year as President of the United States, suffragettes picketed the White House in protest against his opposition to women suffrage. Later, I believe, he changed his opinion and supported them strongly, seemingly a complete about-face. But then, as Woodrow himself often remarked, "A man who never changes his mind is dead."

The terrace where Woodrow and I sat on these spring afternoons overlooked Ellen's south garden with its backdrop of clipped cedars against which rose tall columns of *Rosa hugonis*, the small-petalled, exquisite golden Rose of China. In the center of the garden was a pool bordered by purple iris. Above us, purple wisteria frothed against the iron grill that supported the roof at that end of the terrace. From a low hedge near by came the tangy fragrance of sweetbriar. A wonderful place for a young girl to sit and listen to the philosophizing and wit of such a man as Woodrow Wilson.

CHAPTER XXI

IN THE autumn of 1906 the Army-Navy football game was played in Princeton and Theodore Roosevelt and his entourage lunched at "Prospect." Ellen knew nothing of the proper handling of Presidents of the United States; so she went to Mrs. Grover Cleveland for pointers.

I don't know why I was included in the luncheon. Perhaps because in the President's party there were a number of extra men, naval and military aides, and one or two Cabinet members without their wives. Anyway, I was seated in proper obscurity half way down the long table next to a middle-aged man who introduced himself as the President's brother-in-law, Douglas Robinson.

Mr. Robinson and I lost no time in getting acquainted. In about two minutes we were talking away as though we had known each other for years and I was thinking what a very nice person he was to make a young girl feel so at ease. But suddenly I heard my name shouted from the end of the table—

"Miss Axson," called the President, "stop making eyes at that man on your left. He's a gray-headed old grandfather. Devote yourself to the chap on your right. He's a rich bachelor."

If Ellen were unversed in the rites of official precedence in the presidential entourage, I, still very young, was even less accustomed to ragging from a President. I felt myself turning tomato-red up to the roots of my hair, and that apparently was just what Mr. Roosevelt wanted. He shouted with delight and pounded the table until the plates all down its length danced a crazy jig.

"Mr. President," shouted back Douglas Robinson, "I'll have you know that I'm only a grandfather by marriage."

That was the beginning. And at intervals all during luncheon, there would come that appalling roar—"Miss Axson!" and again the President's fists would slam-bang the table.

Finally the meal ended and I scuttled off to join my escort to the game, who, having made his way past the Secret Service men on guard at the gate, was waiting for me on the terrace.

"What in heaven's name has been going on in there?" he demanded. "Never have I heard such sounds issuing from a respectable dining room!"

"That was just the President of the United States engaged in mild banter," I snapped, "and if that's the way

Presidents behave, I hope to the Lord I never meet another!"

I was still grousing that evening at dinner. "Why should he deliberately set himself to make me conspicuous and uncomfortable!" I complained. And added, "Who on earth would ever want to be President!"

"I should!" Woodrow replied promptly. "I know a whale of a lot about the Constitution of this country and I'd rather like to watch the wheels go round."

We knew, of course, that he was joking, that his chief interest lay in Princeton, where he was now planning the third stage of his educational program.

First had been the required courses of study instead of free electives. Next, the Preceptors to drive or lure or coax those courses through the students' brains. Now he wanted to transform the exclusive upper-class clubs into integral parts of the University life. They were to be turned into quadrangles or quads, rather like the colleges of an English university, where men of all four classes would live together and profit by the contact of mind with mind. Woodrow was a great believer in such contacts. He even wanted to build the proposed graduate school on the campus instead of in lordly isolation on the outskirts of the village.

At first the trustees were inclined to favor the quad project, until the alumni, who would thus be deprived of week-ends at their select clubs, began to howl. Then the fight was on. Quadrangles turned into quad wrangles. We ate and drank quads. The trustees and the faculty were divided; the alumni were largely against Woodrow; the majority of the undergraduates were for him. As were the townspeople, only they, of course, didn't count.

I met a young professor friend, red-faced and fighting mad. "Damn the President!" he exclaimed. He had gone to Woodrow, he said, bursting with a new scheme, wanting to discuss it, and here he was, ten minutes later, hurtling across the campus.

"What did you expect?" I jibed. "To hash and re-hash your scheme for hours? It doesn't take Woodrow that long to make up his mind."

But I felt a sharp prick of concern. Woodrow's mind was so quick, it could seize upon a whole plan while his interlocutor was getting out the first sentences, and then, not given to time wasting, he would have reached a decision while the man was still wanting to discuss. But, I thought uneasily, wouldn't he be wiser to waste a little more time? This peevish, red-faced professor would now be his enemy. Of course, the faculty would have nothing to say as to the final decision about the quads. That rested with the trustees. But if the trustees likewise felt that Woodrow was too summary in his methods, wouldn't they too turn against him? Shouldn't he try to conciliate them?

But I might as well have spared myself the burden of worrying. Woodrow *couldn't* conciliate. In a public address he could bend men's minds magnificently. It is said that, as candidate for governor of New Jersey, he made forty-nine campaign speeches and was elected by a plurality of forty-nine thousand, a large vote for New Jersey at that time. But just as temperamentally, he couldn't ask for donations of money for the College, so he couldn't sit down with a man who opposed him and "talk him round." How different might have been the history of the world had he possessed that ability! If he could have won over the other three of the "Big Four" at the Peace Conference in Paris, or, failing that, if he could have persuaded the American Senators who opposed him to fight with him, it is possible, just possible, that we might have avoided the horrors of the second World War. But these speculations as to what might have been are as futile as they are tragic. Woodrow just wasn't built that way.

For the summer of 1907 the Wilsons took a house at St. Hubert's in the Adirondacks, and I, who was planning another trip to Italy in late August, went with them for two months. The place was admirably suited to our family. Off in the woods a few hundred yards distant was a small cottage containing a sitting room, a bath, and two bedrooms, and this cottage Ellen took over for Woodrow and herself. In the main house there were four bedrooms, one for each of the three girls and one for me. With the arrival of the inevitable guest, two of us bunked together. Downstairs, the dining room opened off the large many-windowed sitting room, and across the whole front of the house was a broad porch which, because of the sharp drop of the ground below it, seemed to be suspended in space, and it was on this porch that we spent most of the daylight hours.

Woodrow's official biographer speaks of that summer as one of unusual strain. The quad fight had reached the boiling point and he was flooded with letters, many of them abusive. There were also letters from his supporters in the Board of Trustees and on the faculty. Above all there were letters from Jack Hibben, and others, who had been frightened by the uproar from the alumni and were all for dropping the plan forthwith. But not Woodrow! Like my Aunt Louisa, he had that hard core to his nature which made him feel that if he were right, opposition counted for little.

The fight was on, and Woodrow and Ellen in their little cottage in the woods must have spent many hours in grave discussion, but we four girls in the main house weren't drawn into it. We were enjoying the mountain life. Maggie and Annie had been given a vacation that summer and Ellen had brought up two strange maids. I don't remember the waitress, but the cook was round, roly-poly, red-headed, and Irish. I suggested to Ellen that I take over the management of the house and cajoled Bridget into teaching me to cook.

Cooking was one household art which my Aunt Louisa had been obliged to omit from my curriculum. Luella, Mammy Vina's successor, wouldn't bother with me. "I ain't gwineter have no chilluns messin' aroun' my kitchen," she would say. Bridget was all for starting me at the bottom and letting me work up through the business, a process at which my vaulting ambition balked. I would start with *rolls!*

I started with rolls. I set the dough and "cut it down" the requisite number of times. I kneaded, and kneaded; I shaped the rolls and tried to regulate the heat of the wood-burning stove. And I failed! But the second time I succeeded. I held my breath while the first plateful of hot rolls was passed around the table. Woodrow chuckled as he took one of the golden brown globes.

"You should furnish strings with these balloons," he observed. "Otherwise they will float out of reach."

The news of Woodrow's presence at St. Hubert's had spread through the countryside and at first we were deluged with callers. They would arrive as early as eleven o'clock in the morning, a carriageful of them, who had driven miles to reach us. We soon settled that problem, however. Woodrow told the maid that when he was at work in his cottage, he was officially "out." And Ellen was really out in the woods with her easel and paint box. The morning callers soon grew discouraged when they found only one or more of the girls at home.

In due course we returned the calls, hiring a buckboard which would accommodate all six of us, driving all afternoon along the twisting mountain roads. A few old friends had houses in the general neighborhood. The Alan Marquands of Princeton, the Lowries of Philadelphia. Miss Ricketts and her mother had taken rooms at the St. Hubert's Club.

Walter Lowrie preached every Sunday in a small chapel within walking distance of our house. He was a Princeton graduate, had been ordained a Presbyterian minister, but had turned Episcopalian. Ellen declared that his sermons showed the effect of his Presbyterian training. They were magnificent. Even I, who had had my full share of sermons under my Aunt Louisa's watchful eye, didn't mind listening; and Woodrow, a confessed "sermon taster," really enjoyed them. But even aside from the high quality of Mr. Lowrie's sermons, the services in that little chapel were delightful. It was set in the very heart of the forest; and through the open side door near which we sat, we could see birds flickering through the foliage of the trees, and the white scuts of rabbits disappearing in the underbrush. Once, noticing a pleased half-smile on Woodrow's face I turned to look in the direction in which he was looking, and saw on the threshold of the open door a small gray squirrel, bushy tail curved against its back, tiny paws folded in an attitude of prayer. It sat there for an appreciably long moment, head cocked as though listening, then with a loud chuck-chuck, it vanished.

On a shelf in an upstairs closet the girls and I found a Ouija board, and carried it down to the porch. One day Woodrow saw us experimenting with it, and pulling up a chair he took over. Very soon it became our favorite diversion with Woodrow himself and Nell as our mediums. Different from most Ouija addicts, we got, not merely single words, but long coherent narratives which I wrote down as they were spelled out. Both the "mediums" insisted that they didn't move the board, or "planchette." That was true, I believe, of Nell. She soon grew bored with the game and when we wouldn't let her stop, would sit with her right hand resting limply on the planchette, her left holding a book to which her eyes were glued. I am not so sure of the second medium! Although Woodrow stoutly maintained that often he thought the board was spelling out one word when it was really the first syllable of another.

Our method, after Ouija had revealed her (or his) presence, was to ask him to send us someone of his own choosing. There would be a delay of longer or shorter duration; then suddenly the planchette would begin to move, and we would all lean forward, intent. Ouija sent us a variety of entertainers. One was a hermit who had lived in a cave far up in the mountains. Another was a highwayman back in the 1820's. He told us that he would take a "hempen rope," fasten the ends to two trees on either side of the road, about eighteen inches from the ground, and stretch it taut. In the darkness the leading stagecoach horses would trip on the rope and fall, bringing the others with them. Then the passengers in the coach would be at the highwayman's mercy.

Another spirit introduced herself as the "highwayman's sweetheart." We asked what her lover was like.

"Did you never see him?" she inquired, and when we said no, the board fluttered nervously.

"Oh, that's too bad," she said. "He was so handsome!"

One day planchette began a steady back and forth march on the board. Back and forth, back and forth.

"Must be a prisoner in his cell," I commented.

"Not at all!" snapped planchette. "I am Captain John Smith."

He told us of Jamestown, of Powhatan, and of how Pocahontas had rescued him from the Indians.

"Was she really in love with you, Captain?" one of us

asked. There came a long pause, then a brief answer—
"Who am I to reveal the secrets of her innocent heart?"

"I take off my hat to you, Captain," Woodrow remarked.
"You are a gentleman!"

Again and again Woodrow asked Ouija to send us Dr.
McCosh and Ouija always replied, "He refuses to come."
Which to anyone who had known "Jimmie" seemed
thoroughly in character. But one day Dr. McCosh suddenly
appeared. He talked at some length of the old days in
Princeton; then: "What do you think of Andrew West,
Doctor?" Woodrow asked.

There was no shadow of doubt what the Doctor thought.
"West will burn in hell to the greater glory of God!" was
the prompt reply.

After a bit Ouija turned his (or her) attention to us.
Strange to say he took a dislike to Jessie and began spelling
out over and over "giggly Jessie, Jessie giggly, giggly
Jessie." This of our beautiful, grave Jessie who had never
giggled in her life! To me, Ouija announced that I would
be married before the year's end to a man named Mac-
Dougal, and thereafter for the rest of our stay Woodrow
called me "Misthress MacDougal." Since I knew no man
of that name, the family declared that I would have to
work fast to make Ouija's prediction come true.

The Ouija board amused us during weeks of that summer; it distracted Woodrow's mind. Yet later, after
Woodrow entered public life, I was scared to death whenever I thought of it. During three political campaigns—
one for the governorship of New Jersey, two for the

presidency of the United States—I kept expecting some opponent to come out with a statement that he "knew for a fact that Woodrow Wilson always consulted a Ouija board before making an important decision." Fortunately, so far as I know, no hint of our innocent diversion ever reached the public.

"Misthress MacDougal" wasn't the only one to receive a nickname. Jessie and I were having a debauch of Trollope's novels and when Woodrow heard us talking of Mrs. Prouty, the "She-Bishop," he immediately dubbed Ellen the "She-President." Also he turned his eyes on a rather languishing suitor who descended on us unexpectedly and labelled him Strephon, or Colin, or the Love-Sick Swain. He still disliked his daughters' suitors, you see!

Another beau, however, added much to our pleasure. Before becoming a lawyer he had been a professional singer, and unlike most professionals, he was obligingly willing to open his mouth and sing at any moment, with or without accompaniment. He and Woodrow had great fun singing Scottish ballads together.

When a Princeton graduate of the early nineties begins reminiscing about college days, nine times out of ten he will end with an account of Booth Tarkington singing "Danny Deever" on the steps of Old North. The old grad will speak of the dimly lit campus, the groups of silent students lying around on the grass, and the shivers that ran up and down his spine as he listened to Tarkington.

I don't begrudge the old grad his shivers. He couldn't have been more shivery than I was, there on that Adirondacks porch which seemed suspended in air between the black sky above us and the black earth below. It was the season of midges, and at either end of the porch a smudge-pot smouldered redly like a witch's cauldron, and out through the darkness soared the words of that terrible song:

"What's that so black agin' the sun?" said Files-on-Parade.

The singer's beautiful baritone voice would drop almost to a whisper, and then, like a fair faint echo, would come Woodrow's light tenor:

"O they're hangin' Danny Deever in the mornin'!"

CHAPTER XXII

AUGUST CAME and I had to leave the Adirondacks and join Miss Thorp, my "official chaperone," on board ship. On the morning of my departure, I was still cramming things into my bags when I heard the clatter of the stagecoach at the foot of our hill and Woodrow's voice calling to me from the living room.

"All aboard! All aboard for Italy!"

I swooped down the stairs and with a few last injunctions from Ellen and Woodrow and a last wild flurry of kisses, I was off. For me the summer was ended, one of the pleasantest that I had ever spent with the family.

St. Hubert's was some twenty odd miles from the railway and when we had covered about half the distance we met our sister-stage coming in. The two drivers stopped to pass the time of day, and I saw Jack Hibben climbing down from the in-bound stage to greet me. I wasn't surprised to see him. Woodrow had told us that he was coming, and

233

why. "He wants me to give up my plan for the quads," he had said, and there had been a look of strain about his mouth as he said it.

Now as I looked at Jack Hibben's handsome head silhouetted against the green mountains, I thought, "Why, *why* are you doing this?" Even I—young as I was and, of course, nothing like so familiar with the workings of Woodrow's mind as Hibben should have been—even I knew that it was a waste of time to urge Woodrow to withdraw from what he considered a battle for the right. As someone has said, "He never attacked big issues halfheartedly nor surrendered easily." I would change that to, "He never surrendered at all." The mere fact that the suggestion to transform the clubs into quadrangles had aroused such a storm of protest from the New York-Philadelphia alumni made him more than ever certain that the clubs should be abolished. The evils of social exclusiveness and special privilege in what was supposedly a democratic institution of learning were more deeply rooted than even he had suspected.

One of Woodrow's supporters on the Board of Trustees asked Professor Hibben, "Are you opposing the President in his quad fight because of conscientious scruples?"

"No," Mr. Hibben replied "but I want to save Woodrow from himself."

"If it is not a matter of conscience with you," the trustee declared, "your place is by Woodrow Wilson's side."

But Hibben didn't see it that way. He was an agreeable man, pleasant-mannered, a peace lover. He hated the very thought of a fight, of the trouble and upset that Woodrow was bringing to the University. Moreover he hated change.

> *Every little boy and girl*
> *Who's born into the world alive*
> *Is born a little Liberal*
> *Or else a little Conservative.*

So runs a Gilbert and Sullivan song from *Iolanthe,* and Jack Hibben, unquestionably, had been born a Conservative. Also he found it hard to understand how a man might be so conscious of an evil and so bent on uprooting it that no question of expediency would deter him. I have often wondered whether part of Woodrow's bitter hurt might not have been due to his sudden realization that after all their years of close intimacy his friend had never really understood him at all. It must have made him feel that he had been giving his deepest affection to a stranger.

The stagecoaches, after their brief wait, were ready to start. Jack Hibben climbed back to his seat, and waved good-bye. I turned and looked after him as he went on his way to the friend who had loved him as few men love their brothers.

I had been in Italy more than a month when that momentous faculty meeting of September 26 took place, but one of my Preceptor friends told me about it after I returned. It was held, of course, in the Faculty Room in Nassau Hall, the room which my brother Edward had shown me during my first Christmas holiday in Princeton. The Continental Congress had sat here after the British had captured Philadelphia. The portrait of George

Washington, strong and angular, still looked down from the frame which had once held the undistinguished face of King George II. John Witherspoon, the great president of the college, Signer of the Declaration of Independence, had known this room, as had the Puritan Jonathan Edwards and his son-in-law Aaron Burr, also a president of Princeton, and *his* son the second Aaron Burr, who later shot Alexander Hamilton in a duel and plotted to betray his country. It is an historic room, peopled by the ghosts of all the great leaders of the Revolution against England, and the events of that September day and of other days that followed were to make it still more historic. For because of those happenings Woodrow Wilson became President of the United States. Had his faculty been solidly behind him, had the Trustees seen his vision of Princeton as a great university dedicated to the nation's service, he would have stayed on as president of the University, moulding and shaping it into the outward form of his vision. He allowed himself to be elected Governor of New Jersey because he had been defeated in Princeton.

My Preceptor said that everyone was conscious of strain when the faculty began to assemble on the afternoon of September 26. The two factions drew apart and scowled at or ignored each other. He said that the President alone seemed perfectly calm as he took up his gavel and called the faculty to order. Winthrop Daniels at once arose and proposed a resolution endorsing Woodrow's plan for the quads which had been sanctioned by the trustees at their June meeting. Old Dr. Hunt seconded Daniel's resolution.

Then Dr. Henry van Dyke proposed a counter resolution which in substance was a repudiation of Woodrow's plan. My Preceptor declared that you could almost hear the silence as van Dyke sat down and Hibben rose to his feet.

"I second Professor van Dyke's motion," said Hibben.

The Preceptor recaptured the excitement as he told me about it. He said he could see a tightening of the muscles in the President's long jaw and a curious pallor spread over his face but his voice was still quietly controlled as he asked:

"Do I understand that Professor Hibben seconds Professor van Dyke's motion?"

"I do, Mr. President," replied Jack Hibben.

When my Preceptor reached that point in his story, I surprised him and myself by suddenly bursting into tears. "Oh, I sobbed, "he *might* have let someone else second the motion!"

No vote was taken until the next faculty meeting several days later when the "old" faculty voted thirty-one to twenty-two against van Dyke and for the President. Woodrow had a majority of the faculty, but after all it was the Board of Trustees who had the deciding, and at their meeting on October 17, the trustees voted to reconsider their action of last June when they had approved of the President's plan, and asked him to withdraw it.

Woodrow had lost, but he was not yet licked. He decided that, after all, the New York-Philadelphia-Pittsburgh alumni whose fury had so alarmed the trustees didn't comprise the whole body of graduates. Like a British Prime Minister who has received an adverse vote in Parliament he decided to "go to the country." He began speaking to alumni associations in the Middle Atlantic states, in the South, and the Middle West. He told them that as long as control of the University rested in the hands of a few rich men who contributed largely to its support, Princeton would never be a "free" institution in a free democratic country. His blood was surging hotly; he spoke with fire and eloquence—and it advanced him not an inch with his quad plan.

But the country at large was beginning to listen to him. Theodore Roosevelt had been carrying on a fight against "special privilege" and the like. Here was another voice crying in the wilderness. Though he perhaps scarcely realized it as yet, Woodrow's public speeches during the two years that followed the trustee meeting of 1907 were leading him straight into a political career. But first was to come another Princeton fight, this time over the location of the graduate college.

Woodrow wanted it on the campus, an integral part of the intellectual life of the University. Dean West wanted it on the outskirts of the village, preferably on the golf course, apart from the roistering undergraduates. He wanted an impressive, towered building with a great panelled hall where the graduate students would dine in lordly isolation, arrayed in academic gowns, presided over by the Master, and on special occasions by the Dean himself.

At first Woodrow had the edge in the controversy. Mrs. Swann, a wealthy old woman of the town, had died, leaving a certain sum of money for a graduate college and stipulating that the building was to be on the campus. All seemed to be going Woodrow's way until William Procter, a soap manufacturer and a friend of Andrew West's, offered five hundred thousand dollars for a graduate school on condition that a like sum be secured in gifts or responsible pledges, and that the college be located off campus.

In the controversy that followed, the line-up was practically the same as in the quad fight. The members of the faculty who had been with Woodrow then were with him now; the trustees who had supported him then, supported him now. But there were two important differences. Andrew West supplanted Henry van Dyke as the leader of the opposition on the faculty, and Moses Taylor Pyne ("Momo," as he was called) took over Grover Cleveland's place on the Board of Trustees. Mr. Cleveland, who had died in June, 1908, had been a warm friend of Andrew West; he had called his place in Princeton "Westland," and had stood back of the Dean in every move he made. Now "Momo" was to be West's backer.

He was an interesting man, this Andrew West. Heavily built, with a reddish, healthy-looking complexion and a genial smile which blinded the unobservant to the shrewd, too-small eyes. He had an attractive personality when he chose to exercise it, and he chose to exercise it often. I was always pleased when I found myself next to him at a dinner party, for I knew that I was certain not to be bored. But to see West's facile charm at its best one had to glimpse a chance meeting between him and an old grad on the campus.

"Why, my *dear* fellow!" West would exclaim, laying an affectionate hand on the old grad's shoulder, giving the impression that he had been longing for weeks to run across just this particular fellow. I myself more than once witnessed such a meeting, and it was highly effective. But with all his subtlety in getting his own way, Andrew West was a gentleman, and I shall never forget that he dubbed the whispered scandal about Woodrow preposterous nonsense.

Now, armed with Procter's half million dollar offer, West began his real fight for the kind of graduate college he wanted. The quad wrangles were almost forgotten in this new and much greater battle. Ellen, thoroughly in character, thought of a poem to fit the situation, only this time it was a bit of nonsense verse:

> *The Owl, the Eel, and the Warming Pan*
> *Went to call on the Soap-fat Man.*
> *The Soap-fat Man wasn't within,*
> *He'd gone for a ride on his rolling pin.*
> *So they all came back by way of the town,*
> *And turned the meeting house upside down.*

The characters in the verse, of course, stood for Dean West, the donor, and West's two chief supporters on the Board of Trustees and the faculty.

Most people couldn't get any fun out of the controversy, not even the mild fun of a nonsense verse. "Wilson should resign," one trustee declared angrily.

"He won't!" his companion replied. "He knows that if

he resigned the presidency of Princeton, he'd never be able to get another job."

At this stage, Woodrow achieved what was probably one of the most remarkable feats of his career. He went before the Board of Trustees and persuaded them to refuse Procter's offer. It wasn't just because he objected to the off-campus location of the graduate college, the condition attached to the offer, but because, thus located, it would nullify the thing for which he was fighting, which was the freeing of the University from cliques and special privileges, the development in the whole student body of a democratic spirit which, he contended, should be indigenous to an American University.

It was then, I think, that the public became keenly conscious of the fight that Woodrow was waging. Here was a college president who was fighting for something that was supposed to be the keystone of the American structure, who had just refused a gift of five hundred thousand dollars. A college president turning down a half-million! What kind of chap was this?

George Harvey in a series of leading articles began telling the public what *he* thought of Woodrow Wilson. "This," he said in substance, "is the kind of man we need for President of the United States."

My bedroom at "Prospect" was in the second story of the square tower, at right angles to Ellen's room, my south window looking across to her west. One night I was awakened at midnight by the sound of Woodrow's voice in Ellen's room. I couldn't hear what he was saying, but

I was startled by the note of tenseness. It went on and on, and at last I slipped on a dressing gown and went out into the hall. Ellen's door was open and I could see her leaning back in a big chair, obviously close to tears. Woodrow replaced the telephone on the table and turning, saw me in the hall. He called me in and told me what had happened. An old man named Wyman in Massachusetts had just died, leaving the bulk of his fortune, roughly estimated at ten million dollars, for a graduate college at Princeton, and naming West as one of the trustees.

Woodrow's mouth was set in grim lines. "I could lick a half-million," he said, "but I'm licked by ten millions."

CHAPTER XXIII

MY NIECES and I took an intelligent interest in the happenings around us, but, after all, we were young and the quad-graduate college troubles didn't weigh on us heavily. Princeton was now rather more sophisticated than it had been during the Library Place period, but our lives were still simplicity itself judged by present day standards. We had never tasted a cocktail or heard of a night club. Motion pictures still lurked in the future. Occasionally we went to the theatre in New York or Philadelphia, but only when something "really worth while" was playing. Even automobiles were as yet scarcely part of our consciousness. But to offset these lacks, we had normal outdoor diversions. Margaret and Nell were good tennis players and skaters. I rode horseback, hiring a nice little mare from the local livery stable. We were all experts in a canoe. Above all, we had dances without end and an endless and ever renewed supply of men.

When we first went to "Prospect," there had been only one telephone in the house, on the wall near Annie's pantry. Now there were three extensions—one in Woodrow's study, one in the library, one in Ellen's bedroom. To save Annie the bother of looking for us all over that big house, we girls had agreed on a system of two rings for me, three for Marga, and so on. At the first tinkle of the bell, four girls would sit up alertly until, the signal having been caught, three of them could relax. Woodrow tried to enforce a rule that no one should leave the dinner table to answer the telephone, but at that four pairs of eyes looked at him reproachfully.

"Oh, *Father!*"

"Oh, Brother *Woodrow!*"

"All right! All right!" He hastily backed down. Then he quoted a remark of Chief Justice Fuller—that he held jurisdiction over the whole of the United States, from the Atlantic to the Pacific, from Canada to the Gulf of Mexico, with the exception of the Fuller family.

Woodrow had what we considered a quaintly old-fashioned prejudice. He disliked the notion of a young man lolling in his room and summoning a girl to speak to him. One day by mistake my signal rang in the study and Woodrow himself answered it. A man said, "So-and-so speaking. I'd like to speak to Miss Axson."

"This is Woodrow Wilson speaking," Woodrow replied, and the ice in his voice must have frozen the young man's ear. "Can't you walk over to 'Prospect,' and ask to see Miss Axson?"

"Y-y-yes, sir!" stammered the poor unfortunate, and hung up the receiver.

A few minutes later, Woodrow met me in the hall and told me what had happened. I recognized the name as belonging to a "Seminole," that is, a student in the Theological Seminary which, though situated in Princeton, was not connected with the University. "Seminoles" were not popular with the Princeton girls of my day, and this particular young man I knew only slightly and liked still less.

"He had his nerve to ring me up at all!" I ejaculated, and began to laugh, picturing the creature's dismay when he found the president of the University on the telephone.

Woodrow looked relieved: "It's lucky you don't like him, for I fancy I've lost you a beau."

He had! I heard never another word from the "Seminole."

It was in May, 1909, that Procter had made his offer of five hundred thousand dollars; in January of the following year that Woodrow persuaded the Trustees to refuse it; not until May of 1910 that old Isaac Wyman had died and bequeathed Princeton his fortune. During all those last months of 1909, Woodrow was still hard at work on his own plan for the graduate college. He had been beaten, but not completely dismayed by the defeat of his quad plan. He still had hopes of a decisive victory against West.

And so the year of 1909 drew to a close. The last day of December found us all at "Prospect," as were two cousins who were decidedly not favorites with my nieces and me. Princeton was not given to hilarious New Year's Eve celebrations, and on that occasion, after a quiet family dinner, we sat in the library wishing fervently that the dull evening would end. At ten o'clock Ellen gave the signal for bed. The cousins said goodnight and disappeared up the stairs. The rest of us lingered for a few minutes, as families do, talking of this and that incident of the day. Then the door bell rang, and in from the icy cold night burst Woodrow's cousin Helen, whom we all adored. Powdered with snow, gay as a lark, beautiful.

Instantly the whole tempo changed. Sandwiches and a hot drink were brought for Helen and the girls and I discovered that we too were hungry. Marga went to the piano in the drawing room and sang a gay little song. Nell and Jessie began to dance. It turned into one of our "stunt" parties, in which Woodrow always played the lead. He gave us the "heavy villain" in a melodrama striding across the room, dragging one foot behind him, scowling over his shoulder. We called for our prime favorite, a Fourth of July oration in which the orator gestured first with one leg and then the other, instead of with his arms. Then he began imitating the reproductions of classic statues which stood in the front hall. Apollo with finger coyly lifted, the Discus Thrower, a Roman emperor proud in his toga. By that time we were all shouting with laughter, and the two cousins who had gone docilely to bed at ten o'clock must have heard the sounds of revelry and wondered. We never gave them a thought.

Woodrow announced that we must see the old year out in Scottish fashion; so we went into the dining room, and each of us stood on a chair with one foot on the table while we sang "Auld Lang Syne" and downed a glass of wine. Then, just as the clock in Old North began to strike twelve, we sprang from our chairs and rushed behind Woodrow to the front door. He flung it open. Outside were the snow-covered garden, the icy stars, the sough of wind through the cedars, and the last solemn note of the clock. The New Year swept in. The last, though none of us realized it, that we were to spend in "Prospect."

The hopes of that New Year's morning seemed confirmed by the trustees' rejection of Procter's offer, but were killed once and for all by the Wyman legacy. Thenceforward Woodrow's eyes were turned toward a public career, although more than one university wanted him as president. I asked why he didn't accept. He looked at me sadly.

"I couldn't interest myself in any college other than Princeton," he replied.

My Aunt Louisa had died suddenly during the first year of the quad fight. "I didn't telegraph you the news, darling," Meena had written. *"She went not like a galley slave at night, scourged to his dungeon. But sustained and soothed by an unfaltering trust, she wrapped the draperies of her couch about her and lay down to quiet dreams."* The old place, Meena said, would be sold, and Uncle Warren would live with Meena and the "Colonel" in the Capital City. So I went no more to Illyria. My Aunt Louisa was gone. The sprawling white house which I still thought of as "home" would belong to strangers; the negroes who had disciplined and adored me were scattered God knows where; and Uncle Warren, an old man now, would finish out his life in his son's chimney corner. It gave me a queer, sick, uprooted feeling, as though the thing I had always held to had suddenly been torn away. I decided to spend the whole summer with my family in Old Lyme, instead of only a few weeks as I had done heretofore.

How Ellen, with her exquisite sense of order, endured "Miss Florence's" where we boarded is still an unexplained mystery. The house was literally tumbling about our ears; from month's end to month's end no scrubbing brush touched the wide boards of the century-old floors; the two bathrooms were old enough to be rated as archeological specimens; the food was awful beyond words; and service was non-existent.

But the company was excellent. The great gods among the painters who had once frequented the place had moved on to fresh fields, but the half-gods who remained were gay and lively and entertaining. A half dozen shacks dignified by the name of studios were scattered here and there—in the orchard, on the edge of the vegetable garden, along the banks of the Lieutenant River, the small stream that flowed into the great Connecticut. The artists spent their mornings working in these shacks, or, with portable easel and canvas, at some selected spot in the paintable countryside.

Ellen, too, had one of the studios. While her children were young she had abandoned the painting which had been the chief interest of her girlhood, but now she turned to it again with an eagerness that was almost touching. She would return to the house at midday, her face daubed with streaks of yellow and green paint, her beautiful eyes shining—"Look, Woodrow!" she would exclaim, "I believe I got the effect that I couldn't get yesterday." Then, perhaps, one of the artists would look over her shoulder and offer a bit of technical criticism which she tucked away in her astonishingly retentive brain. That no doubt explains their decision to summer at Old Lyme. Absorbed in her painting, Ellen could ignore the physical discomforts, and when she was happy, Woodrow was happy.

He usually spent the mornings at his typewriter; then in the afternoon he would walk two miles across country to the Vreelands, Princeton friends who owned a pre-Revolutionary Dutch house built on a point of land that jutted into the Connecticut River. In the rocky fields above the Red House, Will Vreeland had laid out a rough golf course, and after eighteen holes of somewhat hazardous golf, Woodrow would tramp back to Miss Florence's. Four miles of cross-country walking, plus eighteen holes of golf—not bad for a man of supposedly sedentary habits!

After their game he and his host always returned to the Red House for refreshment. Mrs. Vreeland would be waiting on the wide porch overhanging the river, her tea-kettle on the boil, plates of thin sandwiches close at hand on the "curate." But one afternoon Will Vreeland, who had lost the awe of a young professor for his supposedly

Puritanical president, dared offer something stronger than tea. "How about a rye highball, Mr. Wilson?"

"Thank you, I never drink rye," Woodrow replied solemnly. Then he added with a mischievous grin, "I said that I never drink *rye*—"

Will let out a delighted whoop. "Of course! I might have guessed it—Scotch is your poison!"

I happened to be at the Red House that afternoon, and as I watched Will Vreeland's pleasure in this new sidelight on his president, I wished most fervently that Woodrow would let all of his faculty see the play-the-fool side of him which his family knew so well.

That summer of 1910, unlike all their other Old Lyme summers, was not given over to the artists and the friends up and down the river. Every few days, a stranger would turn up at Miss Florence's, asking for Woodrow. George Harvey appeared one day with two men in tow, and the next week-end Woodrow spent at the Harvey place in New Jersey. And then one morning Ellen told us that Woodrow had agreed to be a candidate for the Democratic nomination for governor of New Jersey. She was excited and pleased and, I thought, a bit apprehensive as well. It would mean a complete readjustment of her life. She loved above all the world her husband, her children and her home, and their quiet family life together. Now Woodrow was to go "into politics," a word that had a horrid sound to academic ears. Elected or defeated, he would be in the public eye; his name and perhaps her name would be splashed across the newspapers. No longer would they be obscure private citizens. It was a big decision that Woodrow had made, and Ellen, in spite of her secret qualms, had made it with him.

Meanwhile I had other things besides politics to absorb me. A year earlier the trustees of the University had appointed a new Dean of the College to share the duties and responsibilities with Harry Fine, who remained Dean of the Faculty. And the man they had appointed was the young man who declared that he had "raised that child to be his wife." Soon after I reached Old Lyme, the young man turned up and in a voice both apprehensive and firm announced that it was time to stop all this fooling around, and why didn't we get married?

When I told Ellen, she gave a little gasp of astonishment. Then she laughed—"It's a case of *Selina's Singular Marriage*," she said. That being the title of a story which she and the "Smith girls" from New Orleans had read aloud a few days before. The point being, of course that *Selina* had married the man whom her family wanted her to marry.

I went off to the city to get together a trousseau, but an unsuspected streak of domesticity made itself apparent, and I spent most of my money on fine household linens instead of on clothes. For the rest of the summer the girls and Miss Lucy Smith and I hemmed and initialled my linen, while Ellen painted and Miss Mary Smith read aloud.

When it came to addressing the invitations, Woodrow eyed our varied specimens in disgust, and shoving us all aside, took on the task himself. His own handwriting was small and firm, as clear as copper-plate, and I was pleased to have my invitations go out in such a distinguished guise.

> Mr. and Mrs. Woodrow Wilson
> request the honour of your presence
> at the marriage of their sister....

The decision to be married in Old Lyme was easily reached. Neither of us wanted a big wedding such as marriage in Princeton would have necessitated. As it was, we invited *everybody*, knowing that few would travel all the way up to Connecticut for a brief ceremony. But even so there were difficulties. Ellen refused to invite a certain alumnus who lived in Princeton and who had been especially vitriolic in his attacks on Woodrow during the quad fight. "Not that wicked man!" Ellen declared.

It made me think of the Princeton story of Mrs. McCosh to whom a trustee one day spoke slightingly of another member of the board.

"Oh sir," said Mrs. McCosh in her beautiful, slightly accented Scotch voice, "you shouldna speak so. I am sure he is a verra good man."

"But I've heard him say much worse about Dr. McCosh," protested the discomfited trustee.

"You have!" exclaimed Mrs. McCosh, horror stricken. "Oh Sir, he must be a verra bad man!"

That was Ellen! Anyone who attacked Woodrow was *wicked*, out and out black-hearted, with no slightest tinge of gray.

Again because of our desire to avoid a big wedding, I had decided to have no bridesmaids. So Woodrow called himself my "man of honor." On the appointed day, just as the clock in the belfry of the beautiful Christopher Wren church struck four, Woodrow and I arrived in the vestibule. The mother of one of the artists began the wedding march, and I saw in front of the altar the man who had "raised me," and his brother. When the minister asked "Who giveth this woman," Woodrow replied clearly, "I do." Then, having duly handed me over, he sat down in the pew beside Ellen.

But, as some of the spectators told me afterwards, he didn't stay there. As my new husband and I turned to walk down the aisle, Woodrow, they said, left his seat, bent over and straightened my long train, carefully adjusted the lace veil that had been worn by my mother and Ellen, studied the effect for a moment and then with a little nod of satisfaction returned to his place in the pew. To the best of his ability he had performed his self-assumed duty of "man of honor"!

Ellen had borrowed the Vreeland's Red House for the wedding supper, and when it was all over and my husband and I were ready to drive away, the broad stretch of the Connecticut River was a-flame in the setting sun. It shone on the faces of the fifty odd guests, on the pretty frocks of my nieces, and on Woodrow and Ellen. And in a blinding flash I realized that, just as my departure from Illyria all those long years ago had marked for me the end of one epoch, so this marked another. Never again would I be

known as one of the "Prospect girls." Never again would
I think of Woodrow's house as "home." Whatever the
future might hold for him and his, his young sister-in-law
would not share it. I turned back from the door of the car
and flung my arms around his shoulders and then around
Ellen's. "Good-bye!" I said. "And thank you!"

CHAPTER XXIV

EARLY ONE Sunday morning my telephone rang and I found Woodrow on the line. "Part of my Italian electorate is here," he said, "and no one can understand what he is saying. Will you come over?"

It was October, 1910. Woodrow had resigned the presidency of Princeton and was running for governor of New Jersey. They were still in "Prospect," in the throes of moving out, and already the house looked denuded. My nieces and I had grown to young ladyhood there, and now that life, like so much else, had ended.

The Joseph Henry House, official residence of the Dean of the College, where my new husband and I were living, stood at that time between the old chapel and Dickinson Hall, just outside the gates of "Prospect." I cut short our Sunday morning, before-chapel dawdling and went over.

In Woodrow's study sat a funny, little, big-eyed Italian, looking from one to another of the family in helpless bewilderment. When he found that I spoke his language he let loose a torrent of words. He had come to this country ten years ago, he said, expecting to better his condition and to bring up his children like *signori*. At home in Tuscany, he had been a *contadino*, working for the *padrone* of a big vineyard, but he had wished to get away from the soil. "No good being a farm laborer here." So he had saved a bit of money and bought a little wine and tobacco shop in Trenton. And what did he find? The taxes ate up his profits, and what the tax collector didn't get, the political boss of the district claimed as a contribution to the party fund. He was finding it hard to feed the *bambini*. "Would you believe it, Signora? Eggs cost four cents apiece and bad at that."

"But now," and he turned a worshipful gaze on Woodrow, "*now* everything will be different!" The great Signore would be elected *governatore*; the tax collectors and the bosses would be put in their places; food will be plentiful; and every night he and the *bambini* would give thanks to the Saints and to the great *governatore*.

Keeping as straight a face as possible, I translated the flood of words literally. Woodrow looked almost frightened, "My God!" he exclaimed. "Tell the poor devil that I can't change the price of eggs!"

Almost ten years later, he left the Peace Conference in Paris and travelled through Italy. The windows of hundreds of little shops were plastered with his photographs; in thousands of Italian homes it stood above the family altar alongside the image of the patron saint, and the incense that honored the saint wreathed the face of the great

Presidente. There in Italy, like their fellow countryman in Trenton, the Italians were looking to him to "change the price of eggs."

I have sometimes wondered whether that Sunday morning visit of the little wine seller didn't give Woodrow his first faint realization of what lay ahead of him. He defeated the political machine in New Jersey; his candidate was sent to the United States Senate against the wishes of the big bosses; his seven reform bills—facetiously dubbed the Seven Sutherland Sisters—were rushed through the state legislature. A member of the Lower House said to me, "We spend all our time running around asking what the Governor wants us to do next." Largely because of his success in New Jersey, he was elected President of the United States. But all along the line, like other reformers before him, he found himself up against the same old thing—he couldn't change the price of eggs.

However, we youngsters gave little thought to the future during that exciting campaign for the governorship. Until he got into full swing, many of his adherents wondered uneasily how he would make out as a campaigner. In Princeton, old Mr. Guinn, the owner of the "deep-sea-going hacks," which he later replaced with taxis, was especially uneasy. He himself was something of a political leader among his peers, and, like most of the townspeople, a devoted follower of Woodrow, but the thought of the proletariat troubled him. "Dr. Wilson ain't used to people like that," he said. "What's going to happen when he finds himself speaking to a hallful of roughnecks?" Guinn was planning to drive up to the meeting in Jersey City in a few days, and he thought he'd fill up the car with his five husky young sons "just in case there was trouble."

A friend on the faculty chanced to run into him the day after the Jersey City meeting. "Well, Mr. Guinn," he asked, "how did it go?"

The look that the old man gave him was full of awe, almost of reverence. "Professor," he said, "you'll have trouble believing it. I wouldn't believe it myself if I hadn't seen it with my own eyes. The President stood up there in front of those dock hands and factory workers just as if they'd all been boys together. He didn't talk down to them either—that would of made 'em mad—He just looked at 'em easy and friendly-like, and before he spoke six sentences they were eating out of his hand. Why, Professor, he couldn't have looked more at home if he'd been talking to the senior class here in Princeton. It's a miracle, Professor, just a miracle."

Probably the secret of it was that Woodrow really *liked* those dock hands and factory workers. He always felt at home with *real* people, with the genuine scholars and teachers in his faculty, with the "townspeople" of Princeton, with the war-worn old Colonels in the South, and with the stable boys who saddled his horse. It wasn't just because they hadn't money, either. He had no objection to money. In fact, he numbered several millionaires among his dearest friends. Cleveland Dodge, Edward Sheldon of New York, Cyrus McCormick, and David Jones and his brother Tom, of Chicago. Wealth and social position, or their absence, counted for nothing in his contacts. If a man were real, all the way down to the bottom, then he and Woodrow Wilson spoke the same language.

We in the family, knowing that Woodrow was one of the best public speakers in the country, took it for granted that he would be able to handle the public meetings. But what did trouble us was the thought of the physical strain of the campaign. As a matter of fact, he stood it extremely well, probably because, while driving from one town to the next, he could always sleep in the car. He was taking the campaign for governor in his stride, and getting a certain amount of amusement out of it. George Harvey was delighted with his candidate, and the Democratic state boss expressed himself as equally pleased, no doubt holding in reserve the conviction that after the election he could bring "this professor" to heel. He little knew Woodrow!

At the inauguration ceremony my husband and I sat in a box with the family. On the stage behind the new governor were massed the members of the Legislature, the state judiciary and various state officials. When Woodrow rose to speak, my husband leaned forward and whispered, "Will you look at *that!*"

I knew at once what he meant. Woodrow's well-poised figure in his plain morning coat, stood out from the men behind him as though he had been molded of a different clay. With his lean, long-jawed face and beak of a nose, no one would call him handsome, but as his full-toned voice rang out to the farthest corner of that crowded theatre, I thought of the girl Ellen's description of the young professor to whom she had become engaged—*A noticeable man.*

New Jersey owned a Governor's Mansion at Sea Girt but not in Trenton; so after they left "Prospect" the Wilsons stayed at the Princeton Inn—the old Inn which is now Miss Fine's school—until after the election, when they took a house on Cleveland Lane. They chose the house because of its fine studio where Ellen could devote herself to her painting in the intervals between her not-too-arduous duties as First Lady of the state. Lucy and Mary Smith came up from New Orleans to run the house; the girls came and went about their own affairs; and to outward view the household seemed not markedly changed since the old days in "Prospect."

But beneath the surface, big things were brewing. George Harvey was still proclaiming his belief that this was the man the nation needed for President. Others took up the theme. Woodrow's victory over the state boss in the matter of a United States Senator made Democrats all over the country realize that this new governor of New Jersey had something on the ball. Not since Grover Cleveland had there been a Democratic President—sixteen long years—and the Democrats turned wistful eyes towards this new white hope. Why not put out a few feelers?

In the late spring of 1911, Woodrow travelled to the Pacific Coast and back, speaking here and there at strategic cities. He returned full of enthusiasm for the West. "I'm not sure that Horace Greeley wasn't right," he remarked. "I too feel like saying, 'Go West, young man.'"

The University trustees had been in no hurry to choose Woodrow's successor. The two Deans were running the college with absent treatment from the acting president, old Mr. John A. Stuart. But in 1912, at its spring meeting, the Board elected John Hibben, who, next to Stockton Axson, had been Woodrow's closest friend but who had gone over to the opposition. The two Deans, of course, resigned, their resignations to take effect at the convenience of the new president.

At commencement the following June, as Harry Fine and my Dean were leading the long, cap-and-gowned procession, Mr. Fine remarked, "We have seen academic life at its best. Never again can we hope to attain the conditions that marked the first half of Woodrow's regime. If I were twenty years younger, I'd be tempted to give up the teaching profession and start practicing law in San Francisco."

Now my Dean and I were already setting our faces toward California. His sabbatical year was due, and we were anxious to get out of Princeton where our house in the center of the campus had become the meeting place for all the Wilson adherents. With the opposition now in control this seemed an excellent time to absent ourselves for a year; so we put our furniture into storage, turned the Joseph Henry House over to our successors, and headed west, stopping for a few weeks at a dude ranch in Wyoming.

We were at the ranch during the whole of the Baltimore Convention. Radios were barely in existence in those days, and we followed the Convention, not by hour and minute reports, but by newspapers brought out by the daily stage from Sheridan. When it was all over and Champ Clark had gone down to defeat, the cowboys and the guests staged a celebration. One woman, coming up to me with a magazine in her hand, remarked laughingly, "Look at this! My brother-in-law hasn't been nominated for the presidency, but he has just had an article printed in the *Atlantic Monthly!*"

From the ranch, we moved on to California and there we encountered a schoolmate of my husband's who was now a successful attorney in San Francisco. The result of that meeting was the formation of a law partnership and our decision not to return to Princeton. The older of the two Deans had dreamed of a law practice in San Francisco; the younger had achieved it.

Now of course we were definitely out of the Wilson picture. My Dean had been Woodrow's close associate for almost ten years; I had been a member of his household for the greater part of my life, but from now on we would be watchers on the side-lines. The demands of his new profession kept the once-Dean close to San Francisco, and we had to get the intimate family news from letters.

Some one wrote that on the evening of election day Woodrow had gone to bed and to sleep at his usual time and hadn't known the final returns until the next morning when the colored houseman plunged into his room, his eyes bulging. "Guvnah," he panted, "dey says as how you'se done bin 'lected President."

A Princeton professor friend wrote us of the inauguration—"To me the grandest moment of the whole show was when detachments of soldiers and sailors passed in review before the Commander-in-Chief of the Army and Navy, the President of the United States, the man of whom his enemies had said that he wouldn't resign the presidency of Princeton because he knew if he did he wouldn't be able to get another job."

PART V

-->o<--

The White House

O N ELECTION day of November, 1914, my husband and I met Woodrow in Princeton, where he had gone to vote, and rode down to Washington with him in the President's private car.

This was the first time I had been in Princeton since we left it in June, 1912, and as we stood on the familiar station platform waiting for the engine to be attached to the car, I was oppressed by thoughts of all the changes which these two years had brought. How many times had Woodrow, as professor and president of the University, gone up and down the steps of Blair Hall! How many times had Ellen been with him! And now Ellen was gone. She had died at the end of August, less than a month after England declared war on Germany. Now I could almost see her little, hurrying figure (she was always so afraid of missing the train!) and her beautiful, dark eyes smiling at her husband.

A group of townspeople and a few old friends on the

faculty had come to greet Woodrow, and as we stood quietly talking the president of the University appeared, obviously in haste, a trifle breathless.

"Mr. President" he said, "one of the students told me that you were asking for me."

In a flash I realized what had happened. Poor Jack Hibben! After all his years with undergraduates, didn't he know that this bit of mischief would seem excruciatingly funny to a student?

Woodrow, his manner perfectly courteous and unbelievably remote, looked at him and said just one word—"No." With a slightly rising inflection, as though he were saying to himself, "Why should he imagine that I asked for him?"

I felt sorry for Jack Hibben at that moment although all of us had resented his desertion during the quad fight. He had been so close to Woodrow, closer than anyone except Stockton Axson, and his defection had been at the root of the bitterness which Woodrow ever after felt toward Princeton. That his own people should have turned against him cut deeply. He told me once, in the White House, that the guiles and wiles of politicians which he had since encountered, bad as they were, lacked the ferocious unscrupulousness of the attacks made upon him by Princetonians.

I often wished, after his election to the presidency of the United States, that I could see into the minds of the men who had made it impossible for him to remain as president of Princeton. What did they *really* feel? Those two trustees, for instance, who declared that he wouldn't resign because he knew he couldn't get another job? Were they chagrined? thunderstruck? angry? That they felt no scintilla of pride in the rise of a "Son of Old Nassau" to such eminence seems to me proven by the fact that to this day there is no memorial to Woodrow Wilson in the whole of Princeton. No building has been erected in his honor; no street bears his name. There is, to be sure, a portrait of him in the Faculty Room, where he fought, and lost, his battle for the quads, but as a work of art the portrait is terrible and as a likeness it is almost a caricature.

One of the New York papers sensed the situation and came out with an amusing editorial directed toward Woodrow's opponents on the faculty and the Board of Trustees. "Oh you king-makers!" it said in substance, "You Warwicks! *You* made Woodrow Wilson President of the United States...."

During the trip to Washington, Woodrow, my husband and I sat in the observation end of the car and talked. A little of the war in France, a little of Villa in Mexico; but mostly of family news. Occasionally Joe Tumulty, secretary to the President, would come out with a message, chat for a few minutes, then leave us. Woodrow, if I remember correctly, was wearing a dark gray, rough-textured suit, such as he had worn so often in the old days, with a black tie and a black band around his arm. As we passed through the small towns of Pennsylvania and Maryland, we saw groups of people waiting on the platforms to see the President's train go through. He would go out on the platform and bow to them, but he made no speech.

When we reached Washington, we walked between a double line of armed men standing at salute, into the President's waiting room, and from there into a White House automobile. Secret Service men were in the car with us and on motorcycles beside us. Europe was at war, and over here the President of the United States must be guarded with a vigilance that had never before been necessary. I looked around at Woodrow and laughed.

"At last I'm convinced that you really *were* elected President!" I remarked.

We found Lucy and Mary Smith in the White House, and of course Helen, who, during Marga's absence on concert tours, was the President's official hostess. Nell and her husband, Secretary of the Treasury McAdoo, came to dinner, and afterwards Woodrow and I put on warm coats and walked in the garden which Ellen had planned during the last months of her life.

"Every day as long as she was able," he said, "she had them bring her out here and she directed the gardeners from her wheel chair." And then, in the saddest voice I ever heard, he added, "If I hadn't gone into politics, she would probably be alive now. The strain of it killed her."

There was nothing I could say. I rested my hand on his arm and we strolled up and down in silence. Secret Service men preceded and followed us at not too great a distance, and as we turned and faced the White House, I saw armed guards at every angle. Much water had flowed under the bridge since the night when he had looked down at that river in Georgia and told himself that he had met the only girl in the world whom he wanted to marry. Ellen had come to him, the obscure young professor; she had walked by his side all the way; and then just as he reached the height, she had left him.

The next morning, Helen and the Smiths showed us the White House. The really beautiful East Room, the Blue Room, and the Red Room, which Lucy Smith declared "looked as if it had been buttered all over with cranberry sauce." During Theodore Roosevelt's administration a wing had been added for the offices which until that time had been in the main building. After that the first floor was reserved for entertaining, the second for the President and his family. In the Oval Room, Ellen had placed bits of her own furniture, and it looked not unlike the family sitting room at "Prospect." The bedrooms too—each with a small room for a maid opening from it— made me think of "Prospect." For the President's own room, which had been Lincoln's, women in the North Carolina mountains had woven a bedspread, curtains, and chair covers of creamy white and a rich Delft blue. There was none too much space on this floor, even with the maids' rooms, so Ellen had transformed the third story into a row of smallish bedrooms with baths, where not-too-important guests could be housed very comfortably. That whole second floor, with its brightly burning open fires and bowls of freshly cut flowers, gave one the impression of quiet, dignified family living. No show, no ostentation. Just what the daily life of an American President should be.

My husband had to hurry back to San Francisco; so on the second day we started west. On the train we talked of Woodrow. "I hope he marries again—and soon," I remarked.

Startled, my husband protested. (After all, men are the real romantics!)

"Why not?" I continued. "All his life he has had few close intimacies, and now, because of his position, he is isolated from almost all of his old friends. He needs someone of his own beside him. Daughters can't take the place of a wife." I nodded authoritatively. "Yes! I hope he marries soon."

Early the next summer I had a letter from Helen which was really an S.O.S. She was in despair over Woodrow. He seemed more and more imprisoned in his loneliness. "I can't get at him," she wrote. "He needs to be taken out of himself, to be drawn into laughter. Can't you come on?"

I couldn't go. For a number of reasons, I couldn't leave San Francisco. Regretfully I wrote Helen. Poor little beautiful thing, I thought, she must be harassed to death by this responsibility which has been thrust upon her.

Because of her position in the White House, as well as by inclination, Helen was a faithful worker with the Red Cross. At the work rooms that summer, she met an attractive, youngish woman, a Mrs. Galt, a widow, who had been Edith Bolling of Virginia. The southern blood in both of them drew them together. They became friends, and one afternoon Helen took her back to the White House for tea. As they sat chatting over their cups, the door opened and Woodrow appeared unexpectedly, looking for Helen. He was introduced to Mrs. Galt, and sat down with them.

"I can't say that I foresaw in that first minute what was going to happen," Helen told me afterwards. "It may have taken ten minutes—"

Mrs. Galt was gay and amusing. Woodrow, listening to her, laughed aloud twice. "I could scarcely believe my own ears," said Helen. "For a moment the shadow of the war and his own personal tragedy seemed to lift." Later she and Edith, together, told me of the courtship. A President was not supposed to go to private houses, except to dinners with members of his Cabinet. So Helen had to fetch Mrs. Galt to the White House "to be courted." "And we three would walk in the grounds, escorted by Secret Service men and armed guards."

They were married just before Thanksgiving, a year and three months after Ellen's death. Certain of Woodrow's political associates urged him to postpone the announcement until after the election lest it affect the results unfavorably. But Woodrow, although "in politics," was not a politician. He couldn't conceive of ordering his private life with an eye toward political expediency. The election results may have been affected. Certainly a loud enough howl went up from the country. References to "that lonely man in the White House" had appeared in many a campaign speech. I heard one such speech myself from a Democratic candidate for Congress. I also heard his opponent's rejoinder.

"We all feel the deepest sympathy for our President in

his great sorrow," said the Republican, "but I believe that the loneliness of that lonely man in the White House will not be greatly mitigated by the election of Mr. Blank to Congress."

Women did not hesitate to voice their disapproval to me. "He had the country and the war," one of them said. "Why wasn't that enough for him?"

Strange to say, Woodrow's family approved. His daughters and Stockton Axson, as well as Helen and I, knew that Woodrow needed some one of his own beside him. We were glad to welcome Edith into the family.

3

CHAPTER XXVI

I DIDN'T MEET my new sister-in-law until the autumn of 1917 when I was staying at Miss Florence's in Old Lyme awaiting the coming of my husband, who had been called to Tennessee on affairs of his family. I found that Jessie Sayre was staying with the Vreelands at the Red House and that Margaret Wilson was with her singing teacher a few miles up the Sound. Into this unexpected reunion came a telegram from Woodrow to Marga saying that he and Edith on board the *Mayflower* would be off New London the following afternoon and inviting her to dinner.

We all three went. We planned a little surprise. First Marga went into the yacht's saloon where her father and Edith were sitting. Then Jessie, whose unexpected appearance was not startling, since she lived in New England. Then I, who was supposed to be on the Pacific coast. "My dear girl!" Woodrow exclaimed when he saw me, and he kissed me as he had just kissed his daughters—just as he had done all my life.

Over his shoulder, I saw Edith's face, puzzled, bewildered. "Who on earth is this strange woman Woodrow is kissing!" she seemed to be saying. Then—"Why, it's Madge!" she said, using the "little" name given me by my brother.

From that moment, strange as it may seem, we liked each other. We spent a pleasant evening, and then the girls and I were rowed back to shore and took cars for our separate abodes.

During the evening, Woodrow had told me that they were lunching at the Vreelands next day, and that he planned to stop by Miss Florence's to show the place to Edith. After breakfast I went into the big hall which the artists used as a lounge. Its appearance had not improved since the years when the Wilsons summered here. The upholstery of the beautiful old mahogany sofa was a trifle more ragged; the white woodwork a bit dingier; a stack of sketches sprawled against one wall; a pile of magazines and newspapers against another; dust lay thick over everything. I looked at the place with new eyes. Recalling Edith's immaculate appearance the evening before, I suspected that my new sister-in-law would not view this disorder with an artist's tolerance. I began making a few futile gestures toward straightening it up.

The wife of one of the painters came out and looked at me in astonishment. "What on earth are you doing?" she demanded.

I told her. "My God!" she exclaimed. "Let's find Miss Florence and get to work."

"The President told me not to let her know," I said. "He wants to surprise her."

"She's not the only one who'll be surprised," the woman remarked with a grin. "All right, let's at it!" She herself had a broom and dust pan which she kept for use in her own room. She brought them down. She also brought a couch cover to hide the rags of the sofa, and an oiled dust cloth. We shoved the sketches under the sofa; the magazines and newspapers into the hall closet, thereby releasing a cataract of old stuff which had been stored there for heaven knows how many years. We rammed it back, forced the door shut and locked it, and hid the key beneath the rug. She began to sweep; I followed behind with the duster. Dust settled on our faces and hair. Two of the artists happened along, and stared at us as if we had suddenly gone mad. We commandeered their services to carry off the most ricketty of the chairs.

"Keep an eye out," we told them, "We don't want to be caught looking like this."

They took their stand at the front gate, one keeping watch up the road, the other down; as it turned out, uselessly. For suddenly, we heard steps on the back porch and the President of the United States appeared, accompanied by his wife, Marga, a couple of his aides, and a batch of Secret Service men. Miss Florence, hearing an unusual commotion in her front hall, came hurrying in from the kitchen, her Elizabeth Barrett Browning-like curls topping her blue gingham apron. "Why, President Wilson!" she said, calm as you please. "What an unexpected pleasure!"

The artist's wife and I might have spared ourselves our herculean labor. Edith, not realizing the vast improvement we had made, thought the place *awful*. "How on earth did all of you stand it all those years!" she whispered, as I, trying to impress her, was exhibiting a painting by Childe Hassam.

Their back-door appearance was explained. They had come up the Connecticut River in the *Mayflower's* launch, then had trans-shipped to row boats for the shallow Lieutenant River, and had landed at the foot of Miss Florence's vegetable garden. They departed the same way, with me now added to the party. I thought that the rowing sailors seemed singularly inept at their job. They caught more "crabs" than I had ever caught in the old days when I had canoed on this stream. Half way down the Lieutenant they hit a hidden mud bank with such force that Edith was flung off her seat. The boat was grounded, and we four had to transfer to the second boat, changing places with the aides and two of the Secret Service men. Edith and I looked at each other and began to giggle.

By some unknown system of underground wireless, the countryside had learned of the President's presence. The bridge over the Lieutenant was black with people gazing down at us as we were rowed beneath the bridge. For the first time, the thought of assassination flashed into my mind, never again to leave me throughout the whole of Woodrow's presidency. After all, three Presidents had been shot, and how easy it would be for anyone on that bridge to shoot this President, or to drop a bomb. No armed guards or Secret Service men could save him.

It was a beautiful September day. The salt marshes were already taking on their autumn colors of orange and burnt sienna; the stream as it meandered through the marshes was bluer than the sky; a crisp breeze across the meadows brought the odor of new cut hay. Those meadows across which Woodrow used to walk for a game of golf with Will Vreeland. Free and untrammelled. No guards, no Secret Service men, no intolerable burden of great office. Suddenly I thought of the first time I had met a President of the United States, at that luncheon at "Prospect" when Theodore Roosevelt had badgered me. I thought of my query: "Who on earth would want to be President!" and of Woodrow's jesting reply: "I should! I'd rather like to see the wheels go round—"

Did he still feel like that, I wondered?

During that luncheon at the Vreelands I noticed a curious thing. Here were the rooms we had all known so well during the summers we spent in Old Lyme. Here were our hosts, apparently not changed. But they *were* changed! Mr. Vreeland asked about the Secret Service men who were lined up on the front and back porches.

"Oh, they will eat at their own convenience," said Woodrow. "They don't take orders from me. I'm their prisoner, not their boss." And as Will Vreeland laughed at the mild joke, I realized that deep down inside he was conscious of the fact that the man sitting here with us was the President of the United States of America, one of the greatest positions in the world.

I noticed the same thing later when I was staying at the White House. Woodrow had never been one to "put on side." It was true that he was not the exuberant type, and I doubt whether anyone had ever slapped him on the back except possibly his college classmates. His quiet natural dignity had always been the same in every situation, and there in the White House it showed itself no less and no more than before. Also his simple, friendly manner was unchanged. When, as etiquette required, he had to enter a room ahead of his companion, step first into an automobile, be served first at table, he would sometimes say with an attractive little note of apology, "When my prison term is over, I can be a gentleman again!" But the absence of change in Woodrow himself couldn't disguise the fact that the *situation* was altered.

I think it was James Bryce who spoke of the sobering effect of the great office on a man elected to the presidency. I believe that the people around him are also affected more or less. I myself as a young girl had never been afraid of Woodrow, nor in awe of him, and I wasn't in awe of him now. Yet every now and then it would dawn on me suddenly that I had no business to be talking so lightly and flippantly to *The President!*

CHAPTER XXVII

MY HUSBAND said, "You have been in the provinces so long. Why not stay in the East for awhile?"

"But I want to go home!" I protested.

"There'll be time enough for home. You stay on here and I'll come back later and get you."

So I took a room at the National Arts Club on Gramercy Square, and divided my time between New York and Washington. To go from the one to the other was like passing from the horrific upheaval of a cyclone's outer edge to the quiet of the dead center. In New York troops marched; military bands blared; men and women rushed around with tense faces; every few minutes the raucous voices of the newsboys cried another extra. One day I saw the new inductees of a New York regiment marching down Fifth Avenue. Shabby young men from the East Side; men in loud, flashy checks; men in flannel shirts, in sweaters, a few bundled in winter overcoats. As sorry military material as one would see anywhere. They didn't know how to march. Stumbling, losing step, yelled at by their sergeants, their progress was slow, and their families trailing along on the sidewalks could keep up with them easily—"Look, Gertie! There's Joe, next to the end." "Hi, Tim!" "Atta boy! You're going to be a soldier—" The band struck up the tune to which British Tommies were marching— *It's a long, long way to Tipperary.*

As it happened, I was to see that same regiment again, after the Armistice. Again marching down Fifth Avenue. No longer shabby, shambling recruits, but hard, tough, seasoned fighters. Victors now, unconquered and unconquerable, swinging down the Avenue as one man, while the band played the old Civil War song, "When Johnny Comes Marching Home."

Little did they guess, those poor devils, that they had won an empty victory; that their war was only what the Presbyterians call the "preliminary exercises"; that it would all have to be done over again a quarter of a century later.

For me, between those two glimpses of that regiment, came Washington. Occasionally someone says, "You knew Washington so well—you must have met So-and-So." To which I probably reply, "I never knew Washington at all. I only knew the White House." Vastly different in that autumn and winter of 1917-18. Coming into the White House from New York, I was always conscious of a deep quiet. Not the quiet of inaction, but of the smooth silent turning of a perfectly geared, powerful machine.

On this house the eyes of the world were focussed. Commissions from the Allied nations came and went. Officers from over seas, from our own armed services, members of the British and American cabinets, Senators, Congressmen, heads of various boards. At the center of it all stood Woodrow.

He was taking the war hard. Each time that I arrived, I thought him graver, more troubled than when I had last seen him. One day I found him studying a newly published list of casualties. "Those boys!" he said. "All those boys!" And he added, as on that long-gone day in Georgia when he was telling his small sister-in-law about General Sherman, "How terrible a thing is war—"

But physically, by some miracle he seemed more robust than he had ever been. He had always moved with smoothly co-ordinated ease, but now there was a vigor about his movements that had been lacking before. I spoke of it to Admiral Grayson, the President's personal physician.

"Yes," Dr. Grayson agreed, "he has grown steadily stronger, as if strength were being supplied to meet the great need."

I myself thought that part of the credit must be given to Edith. She knew how to take care of him. In spite of the strict rationing which the White House meticulously observed, she and the chef planned the meals so that the President was fed properly. She gave him the companionship he needed. An excellent story teller and mimic, she could make him laugh. Every afternoon, when possible, they drove or played golf together. She had charge of his personal code, and every day or so decoded for him long messages from Colonel House, or from some other trusted agent in France or England.

Edith and Woodrow went to the theatre occasionally, and sometimes Helen or I went with them. The thought of assassination that had come to me first on that river in Old Lyme was always with me. The President's box was so exposed. A bullet from any one of a dozen different locations could have reached him. And after all, Lincoln had been shot in a theatre! The Secret Service men were on the alert. They were in the box with us, and in the neighboring boxes. Once when three darkish, foreign-looking men came into a box half way around the circle, I saw two guards enter before the men were seated.

Woodrow hated the necessity of these guards. "When my prison term is over, I'll do so and so," he would say. But, knowing that it was their job, he played fair with them, unlike one of his successors who originated a sly little game of his own, slipping out of a side entrance of the White House and leaving the Secret Service men running around in circles.

The President and his wife, it being war time, did no formal entertaining other than the dinners for members of the Cabinet and for the heads of the various Allied commissions. Occasionally Edith went out alone or had a few women in for tea. On one such occasion, the wife of a Cabinet minister cornered me. "Mrs. Wilson introduced you as her sister, and we've been wondering—we thought Miss Bolling was her only sister."

I laughed. "That is just her way of putting it. The President's first wife was my sister." The woman's face was a study. Evidently she found it hard to believe that the President's second wife and the sister of his first could even be on speaking terms, much less friends.

Sargent was painting Woodrow's portrait that autumn, and the story of that portrait is rather interesting. At a de luxe war bazaar in England, the winner of the grand raffle won a portrait, the subject and the artist to be chosen himself. The winner, a rich man, died before he had made his choice, and the Dublin art gallery, his residuary legatee, designated President Wilson as the subject and Sargent as the painter. It seemed a happy selection. They were both highly intelligent men, with a common cultural background, and they liked each other from the first. Every day, unless the demands on his time made it impossible, Woodrow reserved the hour after luncheon for the sittings. The portrait started off with a bang.

Then, seeing it again after an absence in New York, it seemed to me that something had happened. The technique was as fine as ever, but the thing as a whole had lost vitality, as if something had died in the artist, and when the portrait was finally completed, I thought it awful.

A year or so ago I said to another distinguished painter, "Can you explain why the Sargent portrait of President Wilson, which began so superbly, should have ended a complete failure?"

"I think I know what happened," he replied. "A painter must have a definite conception of his sitter. Whether that conception is favorable or unfavorable doesn't matter, but it must be *definite*. Sargent had that in the beginning, and it was favorable. He liked the President and the President liked him. There was sympathy between them. The outlook for a successful portrait was excellent.

"Then Senator Lodge returned to Washington. And you know how Lodge hated Wilson. He and Sargent were old friends; every day or so they dined together. And now Sargent's own friendly impression of the President was over-laid by Lodge's hatred. I don't mean that Sargent changed his opinion, grew to dislike his sitter. But his clear, *definite* conception became blurred, distorted, and the portrait was a failure, instead of being, as it should have been, one of the most magnificent portraits of that generation."

An interesting theory, at least! And, whatever the reason, I hate to think of generations of young Irishmen looking at that Sargent portrait and saying to themselves, "So *that* was Woodrow Wilson!" Just as I hate to think of generations of Princeton students viewing the alleged-to-be likeness of their famous President that hangs in the Faculty Room in Old North. The portrait that this present one replaced was bad enough, heaven knows, but this one is a horror!

That winter of 1917-18 was very cold for Washington. From my bedroom window I looked out at the Monument, dingy white against a background of snow. There was ice in the river and the water pipes in the White House froze. The colored servants, whom I enjoyed because they reminded me of Illyria, seemed to think that they had suddenly been transported to the North Pole. "Lawdy, honey," the maid who looked after me would say, "I reckon the Kaiser's friend the devil has done sent us this heah weather."

We younger members of the household managed to find a certain amount of amusement. Marga came back from her concert tour, and she, Helen and I went to a few parties. But we always tried to be at home for dinner. Woodrow seemed to like to look around the table and see us in our places. After dinner we would sit in the Oval Room, the women busily knitting while Woodrow read aloud. Sometimes a bit of Stephen Leacock's nonsense; sometimes a long letter from Ambassador Page in London. Once he turned to Mr. Dooley's comments on our war with Spain—"Shure, and they say there's enough beef in Maine to feed ivery soljer in Cubia." But whatever else he read, he always included some poetry.

Ellen had been one of those rare persons to whom poetry was as much a part of her daily life as the food she ate, and Woodrow had acquired the love of it from her. So now in that quiet room in the White House, while outside the world crashed and strained with war, he would take up a volume of verse and seem to find refreshment.

Christmas came, America's first war Christmas, and it brought a gathering of our clan. My husband arrived from California; Jessie and her husband and two children from

New England; Nell and Mr. McAdoo and their little daughter from their house up the street; Stockton Axson from his new college in Texas. On Christmas morning Edith distributed the presents—not many and not costly, as was fitting in war time. Among them was a new silk hat for Woodrow from Edith. "Ha!" he said, setting it on his head at a jaunty angle. "I see here the fine Machiavellian hand of Brooke," Brooke being the White House valet who was always determined that his President should be properly accoutered.

The presence of his two brothers-in-law, with whom he had been so closely associated in the old days, pleased Woodrow. The three spent hours together in his study. "I haven't heard him talk so freely for ages!" Helen exclaimed, delighted.

On New Year's Eve all of us were again at the White House. It wasn't a happy occasion. The news from France had been bad, and Woodrow's eyes were grave. He sat a little apart, not sharing our casual talk. After a bit, he got up, went into his study and came back with a volume of Wordsworth.

"Here is something that I want to read you," he said. "Wordsworth wrote it in January, 1806, when all Europe had fallen to Napoleon and England was threatened."

Then in a low, distinct voice he read "Ad Usque":

> *Another year! Another deadly blow.*
> *Another mighty Empire overthrown.*
> *And we are left, or shall be left, alone,*
> *The last that dare to struggle with the Foe.*

'Tis well! from this day forward we shall know
  That in ourselves our safety must be sought;
  That by our own right hands it must be wrought;
That we must stand unpropped or be laid low.

O Dastard, whom such foretaste doth not cheer!
  We shall exult if they who rule the land
Be men who hold its many blessings dear—
Wise, upright, valiant. Not a servile band
Who are to judge of danger which they fear,
  And honour which they do not understand.

CHAPTER XXVIII

I N THE SPRING of 1918, a youngish Japanese appeared with a letter of introduction from the American Embassy in Tokyo. "He is an ardent Wilsonian," the letter said. "Tell him all you can about the President."

Tsurumi was then in his early thirties, an attractive looking man. He spoke English with almost no accent, although he had been in this country only once before, as secretary to Dr. Nitobe, Japan's foremost professor of literature. That was in 1912.

One day during that visit chance put into Tsurumi's hands one of George Harvey's articles on Woodrow Wilson. He read it, and then, to quote his own words, "I laid it aside almost reverently, saying to myself, 'This is my Master!'"

When the Baltimore Convention was in progress, he bought each newspaper extra as it came out. "I would close my eyes," he said, "and say to myself, 'I am a Japanese.

I am a *Japanese*. It can make no difference to me who is nominated for President of this country!' And so, having re-inforced my courage, I would open my eyes, open the paper, and read that Champ Clark had not yet been nominated." At last he could stand the strain no longer. He went down to Baltimore, managed in some way to get admission to the Convention hall and was present when Wilson was nominated.

Now Tsurumi was launched on his mission. He read everything he could find on his newly discovered hero, and on his return to Japan welded a group of young liberals into the "Woodrow Wilson Club of Japan."

Later we were to hear of an interesting incident in connection with that club. An American political writer, who was a sworn enemy of Wilson, was travelling in Japan. He had letters of introduction to this and that important personage in the government hierarchy, the close-bound circle of the old guard. One day some one asked if he would like to meet a group of liberals, just to vary the picture. On his assenting he was taken to a private house, Tsurumi's, and found himself, to his astonishment, at a meeting of the Woodrow Wilson Club of Japan.

Tsurumi had come far since those days of 1912. As a son-in-law of Baron Goto, a former cabinet minister and former governor of Formosa, the political field had been open to him. He was now counsellor of the Imperial railways and had come to America on government business, and also as a side issue, to gather material for a life of Woodrow Wilson in Japanese. My husband and I were to be the first source of that material. When he realized our long association with the President he looked at us with awe, his eyes seeming to say, *"Ah, did you once see Shelley plain? And did he stop and speak to you? And did you speak to him again?"*

After leaving us, he went on to Washington, taking with him a letter of introduction to Edith from a missionary cousin in Japan, and one from us to Woodrow. He spent an hour with them in the White House, "Just the three of us," he wrote ecstatically, "talking together as man to man." Then he started on his pilgrimage. To Woodrow's birthplace; to his boyhood schools; to the colleges where he had been a student and to those others where he had taught; to Savannah where Woodrow and Ellen were married; and to the governor's mansion in Sea Girt which he had left to become President. I don't know what happened to the business he was negotiating for his government, but this assembling of material for his monumental life of Wilson took a lot of time, and before he had finished, came the Armistice, and following the Armistice, the Peace Conference, which Tsurumi was ordered to attend. After the Conference he travelled in every European country except Russia, meeting the heads of their governments, leaders of the opposition, their chief social and literary figures.

When we saw him again, a year later, he was a vastly different Tsurumi. In this country his acquaintanceship now ranged from the presidents of New York banks to obscure young professors in backwater colleges. His Eng-

lish, always good, was now extraordinary. He could even
make puns in English! He spoke of world affairs with a
new assurance. But he still flamed with admiration for the
President, and the projected biography was partly written.
It was afterwards published and, as another Japanese acquaintance told us, had made a hit in Japan.

For a number of years, we saw Tsurumi frequently. He
seemed to commute between America and Japan. He
lectured at the Institute of Politics at Williamstown,
Massachusetts; at Riverside, California; wherever Far
Eastern affairs were under discussion. When he passed
through California he always managed to see us. Then,
suddenly, we saw him no more. We would hear indirectly
that he was in this country, was coming, or had just gone,
but he never came near us. And just the other day, a newspaper referred to a question which he, as a member of the
Japanese Diet, had put to Tojo. Now I am wondering
whether his avoidance of us might not have meant that
Tsurumi had suddenly realized where his country was
heading, and was loath to meet us who had been close to
the man whom he had once called his "Master." He could
reverence ideals, but even in those early days he was inclined to doubt their effectiveness. Back from the Peace
Conference, he had spoken of the President surrounded
by the politicians of Europe. "Idealism up against a lot of
tough guys," he had said, delighting in his own grasp of
the vernacular.

Tsurumi was the first person whom I heard express
doubt as to Woodrow's wisdom in going in person to the

Peace Conference. Afterwards came a flood of such comments. The President's influence would have been greater had he stayed in America, they declared; he lost prestige by becoming a part of political squabbles, ignoring the fact that the President met his greatest defeat, not at the Peace Conference, but in the United States Senate, and that the treaty he had fought for in Paris was bound to fail when America refused to support it.

At that, the critics may have been right, at least in part. It was true that Woodrow was no politician. He hated compromise when he was fighting for what he believed was right. He was too thin-skinned to get out and wrestle with the "tough guys." He hated chicanery and scheming, and perhaps he allowed the other conferees to see his scorn of their methods. Also, I wonder whether he didn't lose influence because of the fact that America wanted nothing from the conquered nations. Had we been grabbing for colonies, for instance, he could have used that as a basis for bargaining. When each and every nation at the Conference was looking to the President to "change the price of their eggs," it was hard for them to believe that we were content with our eggs as they were.

Strange to say, the President liked Clemenceau, in many respects the most unscrupulous member of the Peace Conference. The man's wit delighted him. Woodrow told us how he one day commented on the important results Clemenceau had managed to achieve with a very mediocre ministry, and how Clemenceau waved his gloved hands, shrugged his shoulders, and replied, "Ah, Monsieur, Rome was not saved by *eagles!*" Referring, of course, to the legend that the cackling of geese warned Roman sentries of the approach of the enemy.

An American officer on duty in Paris told me of standing beside Clemenceau on the station platform as the President was leaving for the last time. Clemenceau watched the train pull out and, with the facile tears of a Latin, remarked, "There goes the noblest man I have ever met."

And so Woodrow came home from the Peace Conference, and found that Henry Cabot Lodge was leading the fight in the Senate against him. Everyone knows the result. Last autumn, a man with whom I was talking suddenly got to his feet and began pacing up and down the room. "I wonder if this young Senator Lodge realizes," he exclaimed passionately, "how directly his grandfather is responsible for the tragedy of the world today!"

The President decided that the League of Nations must be presented to the people of the country. Against his physician's advice, he started out on that long, gruelling journey to the Coast, stopping every day for speeches. By the time he reached San Francisco, he was suffering from excruciating headaches, and Edith and Dr. Grayson were worried.

My husband and I took a room near their suite in the St. Francis Hotel and were with them every possible minute. In spite of the headaches, the President seemed in good form. He and Edith and Dr. Grayson gave us spirited accounts of the Peace Conference and of their visits to England and Italy. When they drove out, Woodrow insisted that I sit with him and Edith on the back seat of the car. I hated it. I suspected that the crowds that lined the streets would be saying, "Who on earth is that strange woman perched up there with the President and his wife!" Every time the car stopped, I slid out and climbed into another car only to be confronted a moment later by Jervis, head of the Secret Service men. "The President is asking for you," he would say with a grin, and back I would have to go. Evidently Presidents of the United States had a habit of making me uncomfortable!

Jervis, with his hand on the holster of his gun, always stood on the running-board of the car, almost touching the President. Another Secret Service man stood on the left-hand running-board; a third sat in the front seat beside the chauffeur; still others on motorcycles rode close to the car. Again, as I had been in Washington, I was struck by the trained alertness of those men. They were like eagles poised to strike. Jervis, in particular, was the swiftest-moving thing I ever saw. In a flash he would be off the running-board and into the crowd, ordering a woman to open her handbag or a man to remove his hands from his pocket, and then back again before the car had gone more than a few feet. I could never figure out why certain individuals in the crowd aroused his suspicion and not others.

The President spoke a number of times informally in the Bay region, and twice to large scheduled gatherings—in the Oakland auditorium and at the Palace Hotel. At the latter, Edith and I were the only women present. Sitting at the speaker's table, I looked down at that crowd of men, many of whom we knew, and watched their changing expressions. Just below me sat an old Frenchman openly and unashamedly weeping. The President wasn't trying to appeal to their emotions, I was sure, but his own deep feeling and conviction reached out and caught them. At one moment, as though lifted by invisible wires, all the men in that big room sprang to their feet, and stood for a long second in silence before sinking back into their seats. I remember thinking afterwards, "If he could reach *enough* people with his voice, he wouldn't need to fear for his League of Nations!" But the scope of the human voice is limited, and in those days radio was still a feeble infant.

Before the meeting in the Oakland auditorium, we crossed the Bay on the ferry—the bridges of course were not yet dreamed of—and drove to the football field in Berkeley. The schools had been dismissed, and along all the streets thousands of children were yelling themselves hoarse. One small boy fell off the curbstone in his excitement and was dragged back and soundly cuffed by his father. The mayor of Oakland was sitting on one of the turn-down seats of our car. He looked at the capering youngsters and smiled. "Those are the little chaps for whom you are fighting, Mr. President!" he observed.

"God help them, yes!" Woodrow replied gravely.

That small boy who tumbled from the curbstone must be now in his early thirties. I wonder on what battle front he is fighting today!

Late that evening, my husband and I drove with the President and Edith to their private car and said good-bye,

"Take care of yourself," I urged in parting. "This trip is pretty strenuous."

Woodrow nodded. "It is! I shall be ready for a rest when it is over."

In Los Angeles he did a thing the reason for which reached far back into the past. Ellen had had a friend whose father, also a Presbyterian minister, had died leaving a large family of children unprovided for; so one of the daughters, Ellen's friend, went to live with the Axsons. The two girls shared the same room, went to the same school, grew to young ladyhood together. Then Janie married and moved to California with her husband. They were not among the lucky ones who found a fortune in California, and for years Janie had a very difficult time. Here then were two girls who had been almost like sisters, one married to a man who could provide her with only the necessities of life; the other to a young professor who was destined to become President of the United States. They never met again, but during all those years they had kept in touch with each other, writing once or twice a year. I remember Ellen reading aloud her friend's letters at the "Prospect" dinner table.

And now on the morning of Woodrow's one day in Los Angeles, he drove out to the shabby little bungalow on a back street where Janie lived. He didn't even send for her to come to his hotel. He went himself to call on Ellen's friend. The newspapers wrote it up, describing the rather down-at-heel neighborhood, the blare of motorcycle horns, the swooping arrival of the big limousine, the line-up of

Secret Service men, the President of the United States entering the modest cottage beside a thin, small, woman in black.

When I read it something caught at my throat. "His heart is turning to his young Ellen!" I said to my husband.

Halfway across the continent on his homeward journey, the President was taken ill; grew better; in Washington walked from the train to the President's waiting room, and from there drove to the White House. But a few days later he had the stroke from which he never recovered.

My husband and I saw him several times—while he was still President and later, Harding having succeeded him, at the house which he had bought on S Street, a quiet, dignified, spacious home. But I never liked it. To me it always seemed a dead house. Here he had never laughed and joked and played the fool with his daughters; here he had never planned for the future. For he knew, as did everyone else, that for him there would be no future.

He would come into the room leaning on the arm of his colored body servant, he who had always walked with such smooth ease. But though broken physically, his mind was clear as a bell—and always had been. The rumors of his mental disintegration were without foundation. He would talk with us; occasionally he and my husband would discuss public affairs; occasionally there would come a flash—but only a flash—of his old impish humor. Then he would withdraw into the grave mood which now seemed habitual. As though with his inner spirit he were seeing the tragedy that was sweeping down upon the world, and sorrowing.

He lived in that house for three long, burdened years, and then in February, 1924, he died.

CHAPTER XXIX

BOTH OF THEM are gone, those two staunch Puritans, Woodrow and my Aunt Louisa. There had been always sympathy between them. Their dictionaries held the same words—discipline, duty, faith, the God of their fathers. Each understood the language of the other.

"A stroke of genius, my dear Aunt!" Woodrow had said when he heard of my collecting the young Minister's salary, and Aunt Louisa had vouchsafed him a wintry smile. They both knew that the collecting of the salary, though important, counted for less in her mind than did the discipline for me.

"The child is only doing her duty," my Aunt Louisa had replied.

Probably there are few persons who remember Aunt Louisa's gaunt figure and deceptively mild blue eyes. Even to her grandchildren she must seem almost a legendary character—they never having received the discipline to which she subjected me.

With Woodrow the reverse is true. More and more often men speak of him. "He was a generation ahead of his time," they say. And—"If President Wilson could have had his way, perhaps we would have avoided this holocaust." The president of a large bank, a dyed-in-the-wool, Old Guard Republican, said to me recently, "You know I was always opposed to Wilson, but I wish to God he were in the White House today!"

Did Woodrow think of his life as a failure? I don't know! As a matter of fact, it *was* a failure in that he failed in the two things he most wanted—the adoption of the League of Nations, and the chance to convert Princeton into an instrument for the nation's service. But when I think sadly of all he fought for and lost, I think, too, of that poem of Clough's which he and Ellen, those two great poetry lovers, read aloud to us a score of times—

> *Say not the struggle nought availeth,*
> *The labour and the wounds are vain,*
> *The enemy faints not, nor faileth,*
> *And as things have been they remain.*
>
> *For while the tired waves, vainly breaking,*
> *Seem here no painful inch to gain,*
> *Far back, through creeks and inlets making,*
> *Comes silent, flooding in, the main.*
>
> *And not by eastern windows only,*
> *When daylight comes, comes in the light;*
> *In front, the sun climbs slow, how slowly,*
> *But westward, look, the land is bright!*

DATE DUE

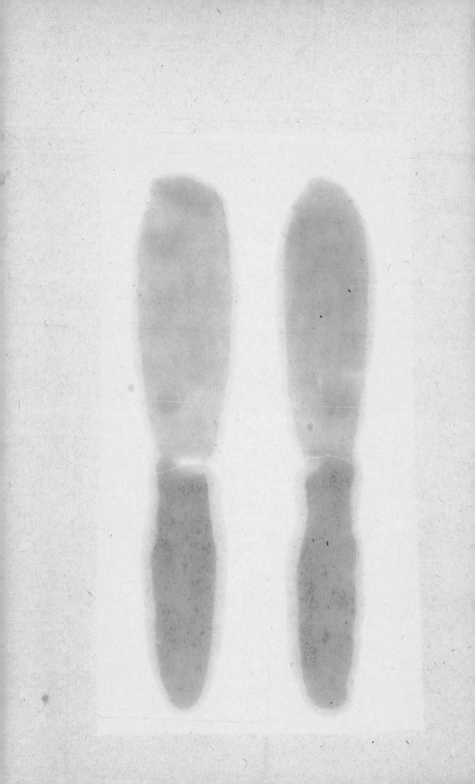